The Best Way in the World for a Woman to Make Money

The Best Way in the World for a Woman to Make Money

*The Founder of
Careers for Women
Tells How to Get in
and Move up through
Executive Sales*

David King and Karen Levine

*Rawson, Wade Publishers, Inc.
New York*

Library of Congress Cataloging in Publication Data

King, David Windsor.
    The best way in the world for a woman to make money.

    1. Women sales personnel—Vocational guidance.
2. Selling—Vocational guidance.   I. Levine,
Karen, joint author.   II. Title.
HF5439.5.K56 1978   658.85′02′4042   78-64801
ISBN 0-89256-085-1

Published simultaneously in Canada by McClelland
and Stewart, Ltd.
Manufactured in the United States of America
Composition by American–Stratford Graphic Services, Inc.,
Brattleboro, Vermont
Printed and bound by Fairfield Graphics,
Fairfield, Pennsylvania
Designed by Gene Siegel
First Edition

To my grandmother, Marie Louise Arthur, a prominent suffragette who cared about her convictions more than that she be remembered for them. May she also be remembered.

To my mother, Helen P. Doiron, whose life is a reflection of fairness and courage, and who never once said to anyone, "I don't care" or "I won't help."

And to my daughter, Ashley, for whom every word is written, and for whom every word is spoken, because she made me care about millions of strangers whom I would otherwise never want to meet and never want to know.

David King

CONTENTS

INTRODUCTION:
Meeting David

Late in the summer of 1977 I was commissioned by *Working Woman* magazine to write an article about women in sales. I had never, until then, thought about sales. My background was the standard liberal arts background, and I'd worked for nearly seven years in publishing before I decided to try free-lance writing. Free-lancing wasn't very secure, but I'd discovered that publishing wasn't very secure either. And if I had to be in an insecure field I figured I'd just as soon be my own boss.

But one of the drawbacks of being a free-lance writer is that you're occasionally obligated to write articles that aren't especially interesting to you. *Sales wasn't interesting to me.* Yet beyond my lack of enthusiasm for the "Women in Sales" article I felt a bit nervous. Business was an alien territory, and the magazine publisher suggested that I interview sales managers from companies like Xerox and IBM.

At that point I didn't even know what Fortune 500 meant. I had fantasies of walking into an interview and not knowing enough about my subject to ask intelligent questions. I was afraid that people would start talking about things like "percentages" and "incentive," and that I'd just sit there with a fixed smile on my face, nodding my head.

I plunged. And in the process of working on the article I met David King. I had heard about this man who believed that women were actually better suited—culturally, psychologically, emotionally, and in every other way—for sales than men. I also heard that he gave a series of lectures and that he placed women with very big companies at very high salaries. I felt a bit suspicious about him and his program at first. Why do women need to go to a man to tell them about their natural talents? I wasn't clear on what his piece of the pie was, and if he weren't taking advantage of the women he was supposed to be helping.

Certainly, he was worth an interview. So I called and asked if I might attend one of his lectures and have drinks with him afterwards to discuss his "philosophy." Just before our appointment I met a woman who had been through the Careers For Women program. She was someone I met socially and she was so enthusiastic about David and about sales that I began to feel less suspicious. She told me that when she left her first lecture she looked at the men on Fifth Avenue and thought, "Those poor creatures. If only they were women they'd understand what an exciting time this is. Everything is open for us."

How bad can anything be if it helps someone believe in her potential? I adjusted my attitude to accommodate this new input. I decided that David King was probably very helpful to lots of women who are interested in what he's offering —sales. Of course I didn't consider myself to be one of those women when I went into his first lecture.

When I came out, however, I wasn't quite so sure. David is an exciting, practical, attractive man. He stands up in front of a group of women, most of whom have never earned more than $15,000 a year, and he discusses careers. He doesn't talk about "jobs." He talks about future planning, and the future he's discussing includes good money. And when David King talks about good money he doesn't mean "good money *for a woman.*"

At Careers For Women I found a genuine respect for the specialness of women. It's refreshing to hear someone talk about women in business without urging us all to join the Marines and watch Monday-night football. It's reassuring to find a man (or a woman for that matter) who finds metaphors for the business world in the women's world. And it's exciting to hear someone with experience say that if you apply all of the talents that you've come to take for granted toward sales, you might have a very stimulating and successful career.

By the time David and I parted that evening we had agreed to do a book together. If you consider the lack of enthusiasm with which I approached writing even an *article* on sales, you may begin to understand the sort of enthusiasm that David instilled in me. Writing a book is a big commitment, and I wouldn't have even considered it if I hadn't found the subject stimulating.

In fact, I've found the subject much more than stimulating. I've learned, in the writing of this book, that sales *does* apply to me. Every time I persuade someone to grant me an interview, I'm selling. Every time I put together a proposal for an article or a book, I'm selling. The business world is not, after all, the alien territory I once thought it was, and much of what I do now could be applied directly to another career.

If ever I do make a career change, I know that I want it to be a lucrative move. I know that I'd like to remain my own boss, and that I'd like to be paid commensurate to my effort. I'd like to remain in an area that affords me the opportunity to meet new people . . . an area that offers mobility. In fact, if ever I do make a career switch I'm quite clear that sales would be, at least, my taking-off point.

The philosophy expressed at Careers For Women— David's philosophy—is strikingly positive and upbeat. I'm convinced that it can touch your life and help you find a rewarding place for yourself professionally. Even if you ultimately reject sales for yourself, the ability to persuade and to be assertive will change the quality of all your interactions. Once you've learned to "sell yourself," you can go virtually anywhere.

Karen Levine
Cold Spring, N.Y.
October, 1978

1

You Don't Have to Make It in a Man's World

1

Where I Came In

I call Careers For Women a sales and marketing school for women, but by strict definition what I began in 1973 wasn't a school at all. As I see it, a school is a place to learn new things, and a teacher is someone who has an area of expertise—some body of knowledge—that he or she communicates to students.

During my early years in business (years in which I was making as much as $75,000 per year because women were selling for me) I picked up my most valuable information by watching women. As a man I was able to see things in saleswomen that they themselves took for granted. I learned that women often don't think about how special and uniquely feminine their approach to problem solving is. My observations were the basis of Careers For Women. I conceived of C.F.W. as a forum where I could tell women about what I had observed in other selling women, and what they might discover in themselves.

I view myself more as an intermediary than as a teacher,

and the distinction is important. Historically, women have been given no reason to trust men as career counselors. Men have been counseling women into "women's jobs" for generations, and "women's jobs" have always meant *low pay*. The more than 5,000 women who enrolled in the program at Careers For Women last year got no such counseling.

Rather, they got support for a talent they already had (whether they recognized that talent or not) and they got pointed toward the 125 Fortune 500 companies that are my clients. I never go to these companies to ask them to hire • women. When they look for talent they come to me.

Some of the women who go through the Careers For Women program decide that they're not really interested in the business world or in a career in sales. But even if those women opt to go back to their old jobs, they return to them with a different self-image. It's one thing to be in a "woman's job" because you've made an educated choice, and it's quite another thing to land in a low-paying, no-future position because of the inequities that are built into our culture.

There's no point in my telling you that women haven't been given the same kind of opportunities in our culture as men. You are, no doubt, familiar with the subtle (and not so subtle) kinds of discrimination that women experience. And if for some reason you're not in touch with this discrimination there are lots of outstanding books—many written by women —that document the social, emotional and economic inequities that define your life. THIS IS NOT ONE OF THEM.

The Women's Movement has effectively articulated the anger and frustration of more than 50 percent of our population. There is no one who has not, to some extent, been affected by the inescapable tidal wave of feminism. Whether you feel positively or negatively about the changes the Women's Movement has realized, no woman or man can deny the *fact* of those changes. They are reflected in our laws, in our language and in our homes. I'm not presenting further reflection.

The premise of my involvement with women is the very same premise that the Women's Movement was founded on. There is no question at Careers For Women that women are as talented and that they have as much potential in the business world as men. In fact, my first assumption is that women are *more* talented than men in many ways, and those *special* talents are the ones that we unearth.

The second assumption at Careers For Women is that money is important. Three songwriters—DeSilva, Brown and Henderson—got very rich when they wrote "The Best Things in Life Are Free." And you can be sure that they were happy to have written a commercial hit. Women in large numbers must begin to earn salaries comparable to those of men before they can feel their own strength. The question of money for women is not just a question of *equal pay for equal work.* It's also a question of professional women earning large salaries because of the special talents they bring to a career. Women are just now beginning to learn that there's nothing unfeminine about earning a great deal of money. As more and more women digest that lesson they will begin to pursue the kinds of jobs that offer a high earning potential.

I uncovered, quite accidentally, an exciting and challenging way for women to make the kind of money they should be making. The "way" has no specific educational requirements, which makes it particularly accessible for large numbers of women who don't have the leisure or the wherewithal to invest three or four years toward educating for their future. In the same amount of time that it takes to acquire a college, law school, or any advanced degree, you could be earning over $30,000 a year.

My personal awakening to the importance of money, and to the kind of talent that women have, has changed my life and consequently changed the lives of thousands of women. In 1973 I converted a charming apartment off Fifth Avenue in New York's Greenwich Village into a classroom. For six years the ex-living room of that apartment has been filled with chairs and nearly every night those chairs are filled with women. Those women move out of my classroom into the business world. They usually begin their new careers earning close to $20,000 a year. Among them are schoolteachers, housewives, recent college graduates, stewardesses, social workers. The women who have moved through Careers For Women are totally diverse in their backgrounds and experience. The one thing they share is ambition and an increasingly realistic sense of their own worth.

My interest here is not to add another volume to the library of women's consciousness raising. I have no interest in *general* discussion and *general* solutions. What I have to offer you is one realistic, practical and specific way for women to make a lot of money. It's as simple as that.

Why Women Work

Women need to work. For the moment let's not concern ourselves with a discussion of "emotional fulfillment." Such discussions have, for too long, been used to justify the fact that women don't earn as much as men do. The problem isn't, as I said earlier, "equal pay for equal work." The problem is that women are funneled into the kinds of jobs that hold no promise of significant salaries. These jobs—all extensions of woman's role as homemaker—are merely one step beyond volunteer work.

In 1974 women earned only 57 cents for every dollar earned by men. In fact, women had to work nearly nine days to gross the same earnings men grossed in five days. Those women weren't feeling the glow of inner fulfillment. They were too tired!

Over 41 percent of the work force today are women, and most of those women are doing tedious, unpleasant, low-paying labor *not* because they find it "fulfilling" but because they *need* to earn a living. Between 1950 and 1975 the female civilian labor force increased a staggering 101.2 percent. The only other statistic that has increased as dramatically is the divorce rate. The United States has the highest divorce rate in the world, and statistics indicate that the rate is continuing to rise.

When you take into account the fact that 75 percent of all divorced men default on their child support payments within the first year of their divorce it becomes clear that it is not "mad money" that women are after but the kind of income that determines the quality of their own and their family's life.

Whether you're happily married, happily divorced, separated, single or widowed, the divorce rate and all other issues that affect *some* women affect you. As long as large groups of women calculate their value at something called "a good salary for a woman," you can expect the same for yourself.

The image of women in the business world has got to change, and the most significant aspect of that change must involve money. Most working women today would find the idea of earning $50,000 a year very fulfilling. When women begin to be paid what they're worth they'll develop a realistic sense of what they're worth. It's a cycle, and I have a way for them to get the wheel spinning.

2

How I Uncovered the Natural Salesperson

In 1967 *Sales Management* magazine conducted a survey of Fortune 500 companies and 92 percent of the corporate executives interviewed said, "We prefer salesmen who do not look, talk, or act like salesmen." It has taken those executives more than ten years and pressure from the O.E.O. to understand that in their 1967 statement they were describing women!

I never set out to be a salesman, and I discovered entirely by accident that I was a good businessman. Like many women, I was an English major in college. My ambition was to become a writer, but I took enough graduate credits to get my teaching credentials—a fast insurance policy against a lack of early success with my plays. (You see, women aren't the only people who are advised to "be a teacher. You can always fall back on teaching.") I wandered around California writing and supporting myself as a part-time college teacher until I ended up in New York in 1966. At that point if anyone had spoken to me about becoming a salesman I would have felt ill. It was much more appealing to me to earn $68 a week as a part-time remedial reading teacher and devote my spirit to "art." Which is exactly what I did.

The manager of The Reading Laboratory, the company for which I worked, was a Canadian citizen, and in 1967, after I had been working for him for six months, his visa expired. The president of the firm and I came to like each other and when it was determined that the manager had to return to Canada, the president asked me to run his business. "You've got a lot of common sense," he said, "and I only expect you to do it for a short time." When he offered me $1,000 a month I became very interested. My impoverished, bohemian life-style was beginning to feel uncomfortable, and I accepted his offer. I had no idea what I was going to do, and I had no business experience at all.

I ran that very tiny company on common sense and discovered there was nothing "mystical" about it. Before that experience anything that was connected in any way with the world of business seemed foreign to me. With all of my "sense" I never had enough sense to realize that sound *business* judgment was not a different animal from sound judgment. There was nothing I did while running The Reading Laboratory that anyone with a good head and some self-confidence couldn't have done. My attitude at that point was probably the single most important factor in my success, and it all ties in with what I will discuss later: recognizing that *the business world is just another part of the world with which you are intimately familiar.*

Women have an unfortunate tendency to back out when presented with a challenging career opportunity. The very same woman who reassures her husband of his talent and potential whenever he feels insecure; the very same woman who employs phrases like "you can do anything if you believe in yourself" when she's talking to her children, will respond to her own opportunity with unmasked terror. She may actually advise the man who attempts to advance her that she "doesn't feel ready yet for *that* kind of responsibility." Remember what I said earlier about the relationship of "femininity" to earning a lot of money.

If you ever expect to realize your potential you've got to check your impulse to back out of a challenge. I can assure you that I felt just as much anxiety as any woman would have when I first sat in for the manager of The Reading Laboratory. Yet I managed to strip the situation down to reality. And I arrived at the conclusion that I had enough "sense" to be able to deal with any problems that might arise. Besides which, who was I to argue with the president of the company?

What has all of this got to do with women and sales? One of my first common-sense decisions involved our method of recruiting students. At the time of my "ascendancy" the company ran a small weekly ad in the magazine section of *The New York Times* to which eighteen to twenty people would respond. It occurred to me that if someone went directly to the private and parochial schools that all of these kids came from and explained to the headmasters or to the reading teachers exactly what we did and why we were effective, we would get a lot more business. The most likely people to do this "discussing" were the two women who actually did the teaching, so I brought them in and told them my idea. And they hated it.

They kept insisting that they weren't salespeople; that they were teachers. I kept insisting that I didn't want them to "sell." I simply wanted them to go to the headmasters and *explain* what we did—nothing more. Apparently the idea became more palatable because they did exactly that, and within a month we quadrupled the volume of our business. Headmasters called our reading lab and asked to speak with the director—who, I discovered, was me—and they expressed their delight at being called on by a teacher rather than a salesman.

I learned two very important things during the first month of my program. Lesson number one was that *explaining* was really the essence of *selling*. Lesson number two was that women were the best people to do this *explaining* primarily because they hated the idea of *selling*.

Women who hate the idea of selling soon discover that it isn't actually selling that they hate. Rather, they hate their image of what a salesman is. (We'll discuss the myths about sales in detail later.) Think about how you respond to salespeople who love to sell. Usually such salespeople place a higher priority on the actual act of selling than on whether or not you're buying their product. The very women who felt least comfortable in the selling role felt most comfortable in seeing to the needs of their clients. And that personal interest apparently comes across in their interactions. If you hate the idea of selling because you think it involves trickery (or whatever steps are necessary to get that signature on the bottom line of a contract) you probably have the interests of people at heart. And if you have the interests of people at heart, you're bound to do well in sales. Those two lessons became the launching pad for my theory about women in sales.

One day I got a telephone call from a man who introduced himself as the vice-president of a company called Diversified Education and Research. He asked me to lunch and over cocktails he explained that the president of his company had directed him to find out if it would be cheaper to hire me away from The Reading Laboratory than it would be to get geared up to compete with our program. When he asked how much it would cost to hire me I said $14,000. That was $2,000 more than I'd been making at The Reading Laboratory, and a far, far cry from the $68 a week I'd been making as a teacher. He smiled broadly, told me I was hired, and I realized immediately that I'd made a terrible mistake. My asking price was apparently so low that he didn't even have to go back to the president of his company for approval. So I blurted out, "Plus performance bonus."

I had no idea of what a "performance bonus" was, but it

had a nice ring to it. He said, "Fine," and we toasted to my new job. I went home that night assuming that I had been hired to direct a remedial reading program, but I quickly discovered that I had been hired as sales manager. These people were paying me more money than I had ever earned before (plus this mysterious thing called a "performance bonus") to do something that I thought I knew nothing about.

Everyone assumed I knew what I was doing and little by little I began to believe them. My first job was to set up a national sales force of twenty-four men to sell the Evelyn Wood Speed Reading Course (a division of Diversified Education and Research) to colleges, universities and private and parochial schools throughout the United States.

If you've ever seen a TV ad for the Evelyn Wood Speed Reading Course you know that the product (the person who runs her fingers up and down a page faster than you can blink your eyes) is hard to believe. I thought about that problem and I thought about the American consumer. I knew that the advent of television had made the American public extremely sophisticated and wary of a "sales pitch." People had learned to equate selling with lying. Every product on the market claimed to be the best. There were dozens of best coffees, and on and on and on. I thought about my own response to the promises of advertising.

When I began to shave I started with something called the Gillette Blue Blade. I then went to the Super Blue Blade. I moved on from there to the Stainless Steel Blade, and on again to the Platinum Blade. The Platinum Blade was replaced by the Chromium Blade and I finally began to use a blade that is so sophisticated that only a cartoon can illustrate its efficiency. You've probably seen that cartoon: one blade pulls the little hair out and a second blade whips along to nip it at its root. The point of my shaving story is, of course, that I'm getting the same shave today that I got twenty years ago. The only thing I learned from all of the high-pitched sales presentations on razor blades was that one should be wary of advertising.

I had a "hard-to-believe" product in the Evelyn Wood Speed Reading program, and the last thing I intended to do in setting up a sales organization was promise a "new razor blade." I was intent on hiring credible salesmen who would make a positive impact on the college campuses where they'd be selling. I was offering what I considered to be a very good salary—a salary that I assumed would attract the caliber of men I was looking for.

When I flew to Los Angeles to begin interviewing for West Coast salesmen I was very enthusiastic. After a few days of interviewing I became very depressed. The applicants were everything negative I'd ever associated with sales—slick, greasy, fast-talking, and definitely not to be trusted. Back in the days when I was earning $68 a week teaching reading I would never have believed that men who had as little to offer as my applicants would have earned a salary like the one I was offering. I was convinced that my future as Director of School Sales was doomed.

That night I had dinner with my best friends, David and Diane Cole, and began telling them how depressing my search for salesmen had become. I mentioned how shocked I was at the kind of men who were applying for a job that offered $1,000 a month, an expense account, a company car and an annual bonus of between $5,000 and $7,000. Diane, my friend's wife, asked what kind of job I was trying to fill and commented that it sounded like a pretty good opportunity to her. "Nineteen thousand dollars a year," she said, "and a free car just for talking about a speed reading course on a college campus!"

I looked at her and immediately saw the two remedial reading teachers I had hired in New York. In all of the excitement of my new job I had forgotten who actually did the selling back at The Reading Laboratory. I owed my new job to two women, but I had flown to Los Angeles with the intention of hiring sales*men*. I was convinced that Diane was the right person for the job. I told her about how pleased the headmasters in New York had been about being called upon by women. I told her the two lessons I had learned (and nearly forgotten) from my experience with those two women, and by the end of the evening she was confident that she could handle the job. Diane Cole—my first saleswoman—was twenty-eight years old, had married right out of high school, and had not worked a day since. She had an eight-year-old and a ten-year-old, a nice personality; she was attractive, intelligent, soft-spoken and articulate; and she looked like the kind of person you could trust. She became my model saleswoman and I went around the country looking for twenty-three more women as close to Diane Cole as I could find.

After I'd assembled my first all-women sales staff I began a two-week training program to familiarize them with the product. I still believed that selling was the same thing as explaining, and nothing in my training program involved "tricks of the trade" or "old salesmen's techniques." Those tricks and techniques were exactly what I didn't want. What I attempted to do was harness whatever "unknown" quality it was that these women had in common and apply it toward selling Evelyn Wood. Watching those women sell actually became my own training program. They taught me, by example, what selling should be all about.

One of the women on my new sales force, Nancy Kaufman, had been with me at The Reading Laboratory. Her procedure there had been to approach headmasters with the improved reading scores of students who had been in her program, and to get the headmaster to write a letter to parents suggesting this program and quoting the test results. Since everything was down on paper, she had no trouble getting headmasters to write those letters. She told me that she planned to do pretty much the same thing with Evelyn Wood. I thought she was joking. Her intention was to approach the deans and other officials at major universities and ask them to write a letter (or provide a letter for them to sign) recommending our speed reading course. The idea made perfect sense to her. The university official would recommend the course in a letter, the letter would be mailed or stuffed in student mailboxes, and students would sign up. I was much more sophisticated than she, and I assured her that no dean would be willing to write such a letter just because she asked him to. There was no way I could imagine her getting that kind of cooperation.

But she went ahead with her plans. She approached the first dean who was impressed with the program and with her, and immediately sat down and wrote a letter. The second official she approached was even more willing to cooperate because he read the letter that the first dean had written. After a while she had letters from officials on sixty-five of the most prestigious campuses in the country, including Harvard, M.I.T., Annapolis and Columbia. In several instances she was given a signed sheet of the university letterhead and told to write her own letter.

I was dumbfounded. I know for a fact that no man could have carried off what she did. Her naiveté came across as trustworthiness. The men she encountered liked her and didn't think she'd take advantage of them. How many salesmen could have accomplished that?

I wasn't quite sure what I was doing, but I was learning from women who thought they didn't know a thing about sales. After a few months things began to happen. The first thing that happened was that I got a $10,000 raise. Six months after my first raise I got another $10,000 raise, and then another. By the time my salary had reached $44,000 I knew precisely what a performance bonus was! Two years earlier I had never earned more than $5,000. My income had increased by nine times because it occurred to me to put women into sales positions.

I left Evelyn Wood when it was acquired by a new company. The new management's sales concepts were rooted "in the old way," and nothing that I had worked to develop seemed consistent with their way of doing business. When I left, Art Kramer, the director of one of our franchise companies, called me from Pennsylvania. We arranged a lunch and when we met he asked me how much it would cost to hire me. By this time I thought I had developed a realistic sense of self-worth, so I looked him straight in the eyes and said, "Well, I always wanted to make $50,000 a year." He smiled back at me and said, "You've got yourself a job. I don't even have to consult my partner."

All of my experience, and all of my savvy had amounted to the same mistake I had made the first time someone courted me for a job, so I quickly added that I'd expect a "performance bonus" if I did well. It had worked once so I hoped it would work again. It did.

I moved to Pennsylvania and did the same thing in five states that I had done for Evelyn Wood on a national scale. I hired five saleswomen, each one very much like Diane Cole. All I cared about was that they looked like people you could trust, that they were highly motivated and had nice personalities, and that they were intelligent, articulate and enjoyed meeting people. And I didn't want anyone with sales experience. By the time I left that job in Pennsylvania my salary plus performance bonus totaled $75,000 a year. I frequently went on sales calls with women and watched carefully as they approached their prospects. Their tone was as frank and relaxed as it might have been if they were talking to their child's teacher. Just as a mother might say, "I'd like to know exactly what I can do to help Johnny with his math problems," they attempted to discover how they (or their product) could help a client. They explained their product carefully, and then they *listened* while the client spoke. I emphasize the word *listen* because I think the ability to listen is as important to a sale as the ability to speak—perhaps even more so.

Each of these women was making more money than she had ever earned before, and you know by now that $75,000 was more than I had earned. You may remember earlier that I said money was important. I was beginning to get a sense of just how important it really was.

A Word About Money

The reason I'm emphasizing my salary history is that I began my career with about the same salary expectations as you probably have. (I actually had contempt for money during the period when I taught English part-time and devoted my energies to writing.) I also thought that maybe one or two human beings actually earned $75,000 a year. I figured that maybe a few more very high powered executives earned $50,000. I never had any idea of how common $50,000 a year is.

Several years ago when I gave a lecture to the Purchasing Management Association of Chicago, the program director introduced me by saying, "And now we'll hear from David King who will tell you how to make $50,000 a year." The large group of women began to laugh. They thought that the idea of their making $50,000 a year was a joke. So I pocketed my prepared speech and spoke instead of how entirely "unfunny" a $50,000 a year salary was. Lots of ordinary men are out there in the business world making $50,000 a year, and if a group of bright, ambitious women begin their careers by laughing at that kind of salary they'll never get to see it. Women have got to stop evaluating their working time at $12,000 a year (or whatever the going rate is for a teacher, secretary or nurse).

If you are average you'll earn $25,000 a year by the time

you're finished with the first three years of your selling career. Many of you can be earning between $40,000 and $50,000 a year after five or six years' experience. There's a lot of money in sales and someone is going to be earning it. There's nothing unfeminine about making money, and there isn't a reason in the world why that someone shouldn't be you. *That's the reality of women and sales.*

When I left my job in Pennsylvania I became president of a small educational publishing house. I had already assembled two spectacularly successful all-women sales staffs, and I was warned by friends that my experiment wouldn't work now that I was in educational publishing. These friends talked to me about the tough competition I was going to meet: the power of the major educational publishers and the clout of their sales forces. Publishing is only now beginning to hire women in sales, and people who were familiar with the industry were confident that book buyers wouldn't respond well to women.

Well, if there was one thing I learned from watching women sell all of those years, it was that a little bit of naiveté was more powerful than a lot of business "tricks." There was no rational reason why what had worked so well for me in every other business situation wouldn't work well for me in educational publishing. It occurred to me that perhaps the men who were so skeptical about women succeeding in selling books had some investment—either real or emotional—in thinking that women wouldn't be able to do what they did. They had their theories, and I had my experience, and I decided to proceed on the basis of my experience.

Once again the women I gathered—all of them modeled after Diane Cole—went into the field and did a remarkable job. They took their job very seriously, and they defined their job in terms of selling books that would *help children learn*. They weren't pushing books—they were pushing education. They drew from their own life experience when they sold, and their life experience proved to be as valuable as the cumulative sales experience of our competitors' forces.

By the time I left that job to begin Careers For Women I was confident of one thing: my philosophy worked. My concept of the right way to sell had proven itself in three different companies. Clearly it wasn't a matter of coincidence that each of my all-woman sales forces had been successful. My ideas about a more palatable sales presentation were valid. And, most important, it was clear that sales *needed* women.

Nothing in my experience since I left that small educational publishing house has challenged the premise of Careers For Women. In fact, I've accumulated more and more evidence to support the natural match of women and sales. With all the companies that call Careers For Women when they want to hire a saleswoman, I have never, since I began in 1973, lost a client. Inevitably, after I place one woman with a company they call on me when they need a second and a third. And inevitably when I send three women over to a major business to interview for a sales position, one of them gets hired.

If you can identify with the qualities I'm discussing, there isn't a reason in the world why that *one* woman shouldn't be you.

Leftovers and Passed-Overs

The more I saw women succeeding in sales, the more interested I became in understanding exactly what their success was all about. What was it about women and about the marketplace that accounted for the remarkable success rate of women in sales?

First, women are more talented and intelligent than the men competing for the same sales jobs. When I flew to Los Angeles to interview for my first sales force, not one of the men I met was of the same caliber as Diane Cole. It was obvious to me, and it must be obvious to clients, that the women applying for entry-level sales positions outshine their male competition. Most ambitious young men are set in their sales careers, and not looking elsewhere. The older men in entry-level sales positions are left over because they haven't made it in other areas. Very bright, ambitious, success-oriented men also move up and create vacancies. Sales has always been a springboard into the boardroom, and the better you are at sales, the faster you make the leap.

The women I was interviewing had never been left over; they *had* been passed over. Every year an equal number of potentially talented and intelligent boy and girl babies are born. Yet when we examine the male labor force and the female labor force it becomes clear that an inordinate number of our culture's plum jobs go to men. Women are beginning to enter the professions, but the earning gap between men and women is actually *greater* today than it was nineteen years ago. More women are working (I repeat, over 41 percent of the labor force is female) but they are still being funneled into "women's jobs," and "women's jobs" are still low-paying jobs.

All of those girl babies with equal potential become teachers, secretaries, administrative assistants, nurses and a host of other things that have grown from woman's traditional job as wife and mother. They earn perhaps $12,000 a year. Many of those boy babies grow up to earn ten times the salary of their female counterparts. And don't for a minute think that they owe their success to being significantly smarter than their wives/sisters/mothers.

They owe their success to their attitude and ambition, and to a society that nourishes both of those traits. Again, there's no need to dwell here on the inequities of our culture. My interest in discussing these inequities is to point out how a woman can cash in on a history of discrimination.

The women who are entering sales today are no less

talented than most of the men who were directed into the professions. The women who are entering sales today are no less motivated than most of the men who were directed into the professions. Those women entering sales today have recently discovered the extent to which they've been passed over by our culture. They're discovering their potential—not reconciling themselves to their failure. Since women are a new image in sales, they don't have the burden of the "old" image of sales. They aren't met with the same skepticism as salesmen because they don't have a history of trickery and slippery deals to combat. This *clean slate* accounted for my Evelyn Wood saleswoman's ability to get letters recommending her product from sixty-five university officials.

When women join a sales force they shine. Their style, intelligence and attitude evoke an atmosphere of class that clients respond to.

CHAPTER

3

What Makes a Saleswoman?

Everything that I believe about women, about women in business, and particularly about women in sales is the direct result of my own experience. I know that women are a great untapped source of natural sales talent because I spent years watching women who had never sold before enter their first sales position and proceed to outsell all of the "professional salesmen" on their force. Those women may not have known what it was that they were doing right, but the men who hired them were more interested in the results of their work than in the reasons for their success. We don't have to understand the whys: it is irrefutable that women in sales work! The born salesman isn't a man at all—she's a woman.

For the moment forget anything you think you know about sales. Forget the men in loud plaid suits who always manage to get their foot stuck in your door; forget those ugly black suitcases that rumble along the sidewalk on casters; forget the word *salesman*.

For the average person, "selling" evokes either one of the

images I've just told you to forget or the vision of a neat little lady standing behind the counter of a local shop. Since women generally have limited access to the world of big business, they have a particularly erroneous view of sales. When we think of "selling," we think of a car dealer in sunglasses promising to match the best deal you can get from anyone else and even do you $100 better. Clearly, this life-style doesn't sound very appealing. But these jobs have as little to do with "sales" as ambulance chasing has to do with law. The door-to-door salesmen that we see as consumers are often at the very bottom of the sales barrel with regard to status and earnings. They have absolutely nothing to do with you or your future.

The better sales jobs involve dealing with business executives or up-scale consumers. The people who hold these jobs earn both a guaranteed "base" salary and an "incentive" (or commission) based on their sales. Their work provides a stimulating challenge: the possibility (but not the necessity) of travel and access to the most powerful people in the community. Unless you're a business executive, it's unlikely that you have a real appreciation of the clout, the class, the power and the financial potential of a career in sales.

Think about it. Can you describe the people who sell advertising space for magazines like *Fortune, Reader's Digest, People* or *Esquire?* You may not even know what "selling space" means, but you'll learn. Hundreds of people are selling advertising space today and making big money doing it; and more and more of those people are former housewives, teachers, nurses and secretaries. Do you know what the average Pitney-Bowes or NCR sales representative looks like? When businesses spend tens of thousands of dollars on an IBM computer system they surely don't deal with a man in a loud plaid suit and a sample case on wheels. They usually deal with men in three-piece pinstripe suits. (But more and more they are dealing with women.)

Do you think you could identify the commercial real

estate salesperson from a lineup of top business executives? Or didn't you know that commercial real estate agents were different from residential real estate agents? They make more money and live in a different world, and that world is beginning to be populated by women.

Let's have a look at what the world of sales has meant to Alice Cummings. She spent the first ten years of her marriage raising her four children. Her days were filled with the tasks of motherhood and homemaking. Usually by the time lunch rolled around she had done a load of laundry and then cut the crusts off eight pieces of white bread. (Her kids were "fussy" eaters.) Her own lunch usually consisted of whatever was left over on her children's plates. She was always in too much of a hurry to take time with her personal needs.

After Alice's marriage ended, earning a living took priority over trimming the crust off bread. She needed to work, and she needed to earn a *real* salary. Today Alice is one of very few women selling electronic components. At least three times a week she lunches in one of New York's finest restaurants, where she entertains clients from all over the world. When she has to fly to Los Angeles her company sends her first class, and she stays in the Beverly Hills Hotel. Until recently she hasn't done much traveling. Her company provided her with a car and a gasoline allowance. Now that her children are older she feels more comfortable with the idea of travel. This year she'll combine her first European sales excursion with a vacation in the Greek islands.

Alice's transformation isn't a one-in-a-million Cinderella story. A highly paid representative of National Cash Register probably sold your local store the cash register on which your local "salesgirls" ring up their sales. A highly paid representative of Burlington Mills may have sold the black vinyl fabric to the manufacturer of the suitcase that some poor "schlepper" is carrying from door to door. A highly paid representative of

Union Carbide probably sold Avon Cosmetics the raw materials that went into the products presented by your neighborhood's Avon Lady. And a highly paid representative of Squibb Pharmaceuticals may have sold a pharmacist the aspirin that the Avon Lady takes when she gets home and tries to pay her bills.

The people who did the selling that made the retail selling possible are the people you need to learn something about. They dispel the myth that selling is some dreadful combination of "Avon calling" and Willy Loman dying. The more of them you meet, the better you'll understand that selling is the single most important aspect of business. It's a good place to be, and it has traditionally been the primary springboard into management. When you think sales, think executives. It's a fact that more women will enter the executive boardroom through the "sales" door than from graduate programs in law and business combined.

Sales Is a "People Business"

More than any other aspect of the business world, sales involves dealing on a one-to-one level with other people. It involves giving information in a comfortable environment; entertaining on a company expense account; discovering people's business needs and devising ways to meet them; establishing contacts and friendly relationships and being informative and persuasive. You don't *learn* how to *have* sales talent. You *learn* how to *use* the talent if you already have it. If you're a born salesperson—if you have the natural inclination and a "way" with people—someone can help you harness your abilities.

Sales managers are usually very result-oriented people. If women had a better bottom line, men were perfectly willing to hire more women. Each time I saw a woman embark on her

first sales job and outsell the men on her force I tried to understand exactly what it was she was doing right. Like the sales
managers I dealt with, I was interested in the bottom line, but
because of my own background I was intrigued with the phe-
nomenon of women in sales. After managing three all-women
sales forces and placing thousands of women in high-paying
sales positions I've got some answers.

The fact is that in our culture women are better trained
to deal with people than men are. Women tend to see to social
obligations, while men "take care of business." Women are
"nurturers," while men are "breadwinners." Both men and
women prefer to discuss their problems with women.

Consider this: if the average man goes to a cocktail
party and the man standing next to him has no interest in professional sports they will struggle for fifteen or twenty minutes
and then give up before they can find a second subject to discuss comfortably. Women have no difficulty with social talk.
Women go to cocktail parties to visit—not to drink. Men
don't chat on the phone. They call for a purpose and when the
purpose is accomplished they hang up. Women say, when they
want to see each other, "Why don't you come over so we can
talk." Men say, "Why don't you come over and we'll watch
the game together?" That's their idea of visiting.

Much of the traditional "macho" paraphernalia inhibits
tenderness and softness and, ultimately, inhibits relationships.
The very fact that women are unburdened by such paraphernalia makes them more open to relationships, and this sort
of *openness* is a valuable asset in sales.

This social *ease* is only one aspect of what I have identified as women's cultural "heritage." (We'll discuss the other
components in more detail later.) This heritage is a valuable
commodity, and getting in touch with it—understanding that
the very things that make you different from men are your
greatest assets—may qualify you to enter the business world

as a saleswoman with big first year's earnings even if you've never worked a day in your life.

You don't have to learn to act like men, to talk like men, or to think like men to be successful in sales. In fact, trying to talk, act and think like a man is the first step on your way to nowhere.

Apples and Oranges

You may remember the old math problem of apples and oranges, explained by your second-grade teacher. As I recall, one couldn't add apples with oranges because they were two distinctly different fruits. Your second-grade teacher probably explained that while you couldn't add apples and oranges, you *could* find the common denominator—which in this instance is "fruit"—and then do your addition. So now you can say that six apples and three oranges equal nine fruits.

Since you probably had your fill of this problem in second grade, let me bring you up to date with its modern-day application. Ask yourself which is better, apples or oranges. Fortunately there is no answer to that question. Each fruit has its own unique qualities and it's a wise apple that doesn't try and pass itself off as an orange. Of course, if your intention is to make a good pie you'd best not try to do it with oranges. Oranges just don't have the *natural qualities* that go into the making of a good fruit pie.

Women and men are like apples and oranges in that they belong to the same species (*Homo sapiens*), in that neither one is objectively better than the other, and, finally, in that men and women each have certain *natural qualities* that make them better at some things than at others.

Yet most eight-year-old boys will tell you, without even being asked, that boys are better than girls. Unfortunately, I know lots of adults who never quite moved beyond that belief.

In fact, history has tampered with women's perception of themselves so much that lots of women today agree on some unconscious level with their eight-year-old sons' assessment. The distortion of femininity has created a whopping female inferiority complex, and if you don't believe this applies to you, consider the following.

* What conclusions do you draw about a man who plans his life around a career in which his maximum earning potential is $15,000 a year? I conclude that such a man doesn't set a very high value on himself.

* What conclusions do you draw about men who tell their future employers that they aren't interested in salary but only want to "love" what they're doing? I'd conclude that a man who essentially tells his employer not to offer him a high salary doesn't have much on the ball.

* What conclusions do you draw about a man who, offered the opportunity of advancement, tells his boss that he really doesn't think he's ready to handle the new responsibility?

I don't think there's anything off-target about my conclusions, and I know from my own business experience that women do those sorts of things all the time. Women have spent so long digesting their negative image that the very concept of "what is feminine" has been distorted. Somehow it became feminine to stay in the background, to earn a low salary, and to clear the way for men to attain positions of power. Somehow all of the things that we'd consider stupid for a man to do are considered "feminine" when a woman does them.

The other side of this coin is even worse. Many female character strengths—things that make women different from men—have been defined as weaknesses. Emotional frankness, for example, has been labeled "sentimentality." And a lack of rigidity has been misnomered "indecisiveness."

Clearly, once you're finished defining women's strengths

as weaknesses, and their weaknesses as strengths, there's not much left for ambitious women to do but look elsewhere for their definition. Unfortunately, women today are being advised that in order to succeed in business they need to begin acting like men. Nothing could be further from the truth.

A woman who attempts to talk, think and act like a man is bound to be a "bad apple." Whatever it is that women do, they do it best when they can draw from their unique experience as women—when they can work within the framework of their cultural heritage—and be themselves. Once women get in touch with what their real strengths are they can begin to apply those strengths.

I'm convinced that women belong in sales just as naturally as apples belong in pies. Nothing could be more American.

Back to Nature

Part of what's wrong with the way women see their role in the business world is that they have learned about the business world from men. They have learned from men that business is a *man's world*. Not a very inviting label, is it? The message historically conveyed to women about business has been DO NOT ENTER, and sales, more than any other aspect of business, has traditionally been dominated by men.

It's staggering to imagine the number of women who have succumbed to the myth of sales as a "man's world" without even testing the water themselves. When you consider how difficult life in the business world has been for women—the psychological hurdles they have had to leap—it's miraculous that anyone has been successful. Those women who have made it in sales have made it because of their talent, their determination, and because they were able to break through the myth of sales as being a man's world.

When I began approaching sales managers and explaining why I thought they should begin to hire women, nearly all of them had the same four questions:

What about menstruation?

What about menopause?

What about sexual promiscuity?

What about pregnancy?

I heard these same questions so frequently that I began to refer to them as the Four Horsemen of the Apocalypse. Obviously, once these men began hiring women they discovered that, despite any medieval literature they may have read, the crops didn't fail in the presence of menstruating women.

But even though some men can deal with their irrational anxieties about women, the sales arena is still suffused with subtle chauvinism. (Later I'll discuss ways in which women can make some of this "chauvinism" work *for* them rather than *against* them, but no woman should ever plan her career around the attitude of men—whether it's supportive or chauvinistic.)

Let's go back to the message of exclusivity conveyed by the phrase "man's world." How comfortable can a woman expect to feel in a man's world? It's crucial to separate myth from reality. "Man's world" is myth. Reality—when we talk about sales—involves performance. The most chauvinistic sales manager will alter his views if confronted with a saleswoman who knows her product and understands where it is needed. It happens every day.

In fact, the sales world belongs to people who sell, regardless of their gender. You don't need to start watching Monday Night Football or enlist in the Marines in order to understand the dynamics of sales. You need only keep your eyes and ears open wherever you are and whatever you're doing. Life experience can generally translate into sales acumen if you recognize its value and trust your instincts. If you can organize a fund-raiser, get along with people, teach a friend a difficult recipe, and keep your kids from killing each other, then you may have the potential to earn big money in sales.

Just Like a Woman

I once went on a sales call with a woman I supervised. She noticed that the client had a book about gourmet cooking on his desk, and after the initial introductions she mentioned that she was interested in Chinese cooking. She and the man we were calling on spent nearly a half hour discussing the availability of fresh ginger, the pros and cons of iron vs. aluminum woks, and the various courses in Oriental cooking available in San Francisco—while I sat fidgeting in my seat waiting for the sales presentation to begin. Finally, they got around to the matter at hand and concluded an impressive sales negotiation in less than five minutes. When we left the building the saleswoman turned to me and said, "David, if you're going to fidget and look at your watch while I'm giving my sales presentation I'm not going to bring you around with me anymore!" So much for Monday Night Football.

Once women begin to view sales, and all business for that matter, as another aspect of the world in which they live, rather than an alien planet, they will be able to draw from the well of their own experience while making business decisions. If a woman in sales feels uncomfortable with some aspect of her job it's entirely likely that there's something wrong with the job, not with her.

Joan Dunne discovered, shortly after she began her first sales job, that she had to carry around a big black box—yes, the kind you roll along the sidewalk on casters—filled with men's hosiery. After her first week on the job she called me to say that she was going to quit. She simply couldn't go on lugging "this ugly, noisy, tacky-looking box around." She liked dealing with people and discussing her product, but the prospect of wheeling her suitcase around town depressed her. I asked her to wait one more day before she resigned and that night I went up to her apartment. She had a small Louis Vuitton attaché case—about three inches thick—and the two of us spent several hours cutting socks in half and pasting them to flat pieces of cardboard. By the time we finished cutting and pasting we had arranged her entire sample kit so that it fit into the attaché case. She was the only woman on her sales staff and she was the only person to have felt genuinely disturbed by the "baggage" of her job. The men she worked with thought she was behaving "just like a woman." But by the end of her first six months in sales she was selling more merchandise than any of her fellow sales representatives, and her clients liked the image she projected. If the sales manager thought her emotional response to the "big black box" was a joke when she first voiced it he was no longer laughing when she placed her orders. She was indeed acting like a woman: a smart woman who knows what she needs to feel comfortable.

Once Joan recognized that sales was a part of her own world she was able to adjust the contents of the big black box to suit her own style. The most important change in attitude —the change that will initiate all other changes—must be in the heads of the women entering sales. The man who hires you has no idea of how much you actually have to offer until you begin offering. Looking to him for your image will maintain the status quo, and the status quo of the sales image is in dire need of an overhaul. There are probably lots of salesmen today who are carrying their samples in a sleek, thin, dignified attaché case because they learned how to "think like a woman."

Earlier I discussed *social ease* as one aspect of women's cultural "heritage." Clearly this *ease* is a valuable asset in a people-oriented area like sales. Let's consider other things that come naturally to women that might account for their success in the field.

The old salesman sounds like he's said it all so often that

even *he* doesn't believe it anymore. Women are more open and candid than men. They're less afraid to admit their own weaknesses and they're not involved with defending a macho image. Women are allowed to be vulnerable; allowed to ask for help. They listen better and create a completely different kind of climate for buyers.

I once placed a woman named Eileen with a company that sells business machines. One of her first clients had a terrible cold when she called on him. She spoke for a few minutes and interrupted herself by saying that she really felt uncomfortable trying to sell him a fleet of typewriters when all she could think about was how awful he must be feeling. He was enormously appreciative; she called a few days later to see how he was doing and they set up an appointment. By the time of the second meeting a certain degree of trust was already established and she made a sale.

A man reading about Eileen's experience might think that she used smart sales strategy. In fact, strategy had nothing to do with the way she sold her typewriters. She was simply responding to the situation *like a woman*. Women don't approach buyers as "prospective sales." They approach them as people. When Eileen met her client she didn't see an order sheet; she saw a man with a cold and that's what she responded to.

Women who devote their energies to acting like men run the risk of losing the very traits that are most accountable for their success. A man in Eileen's place would probably have felt sympathetic to the client's discomfort but would have responded by attempting to speed things up and finish the sale. It's unlikely that that sort of approach would have had the long-range impact (even if a sale were made) that Eileen's approach had. She was establishing a relationship.

It may be required, when you get your first sales job, that you take a sales training course sponsored by your new company. There are valuable things to be learned in such programs

—particularly information about your product—but in order to profit from them you have to learn to *feminize* their information. Don't ever do anything in a sales presentation that doesn't feel like you. Since sales representatives have traditionally been men, some of the things you learn—the techniques you're advised to use—are geared to men. You have to listen with a keen ear, and most large companies will appreciate your input. If you're among the first women they've hired in sales positions, then they're probably feeling at least as nervous as you are. Hopefully they'll learn as much from the women they hire as I did.

Women's Intuition

Another aspect of trusting your own instincts in sales involves recognizing the value of your life experience and how it applies *directly* to what you'll be doing. Ironically, many of the skills important to selling—like the ability to digest and communicate information—are skills that women have traditionally applied to teaching careers. Education is, of course, another area with very low earning potential; a woman's area. But when you apply teaching skills to sales you can begin to make BIG money. Consider Sue Salko, a sales representative for Western Union.

The absolute truth of the matter is that if someone had told me five years ago—even a year and a half ago —that I would be a saleswoman I would have laughed. A saleswoman! It would have sounded like an insult to me. I was a dancer—I'd danced with the Metropolitan Opera. I was an artist. And at my most banal, I was a teacher. But even as a teacher I was into something special. I taught body movement for several adult education programs. As far as I knew, salespeople were sleazy, slimy,

*overbearing men in doubleknit suits; which is a terrible
thing for me to say because my own father was a salesman. He wasn't sleazy but he traveled so much that I
almost never got to see him.*

*God I was naive. I'm forty-five years old, I have
three teenage kids, I have a B.A. in Physical Education
and I have an M.A. in Guidance. And with all of those
degrees and all of that life experience, until this year I
never earned more than $8,000. This year I sold Mail-a-
gram packages for Western Union and I made just under
$20,000. And I'm just beginning. I'm a saleswoman. But
the incredible thing is that I finally realized that I'd always been a saleswoman. I just never knew it. The fact
that I literally didn't know what I was doing has cost me
thousands and thousands of dollars over the years.*

For years I went out and explained *to school systems why they should let me teach my course on body
movement in their adult education programs. If you had
asked me then what I did, I would have said I was a
teacher.* I was selling.

*When my kids were small I put together a sort of
dancing clown act—we called it "Simply a Clown"—and
I got us booked in every school within a sixty-mile radius
of my home. If you had asked me then what I did I would
have said I was a dancer.* I was selling.

*Now I approach businesses that use Western Union
Mail-a-grams and I* inform *them that because of the
quantity of their business they don't have to pay the same
rates as the average individual. I "explain" that for a flat
annual fee they can have limitless use of our services and
save money in the long run. They thank me. And if they
ask me what I'm doing I'll say right out that I'm selling.*

*I'm not inexperienced at doing what I do. I'm just
inexperienced at doing it for money. Now that I'm earn-*

*ing $20,000 a year I've discovered that it's a lot more fun
to sell for money than it is to sell by some other name for
no money.*

The more I learned about sales, the more I recognized its
far-reaching implications. Teaching isn't the only traditionally
female job that relates directly to selling. Many women, in
many fields, get a somewhat déjà vu feeling when they learn
about sales.

To whatever extent your activity involves dealing with
people on a one-to-one basis, your experiences will help you
in your new career. Even when you manage to convince your
friends to eat Chinese food rather than Italian food, you're
preparing for a career in sales. And whatever it is that you
want to do you're likely to do it better if you have a sales
background.

Every book that's published today about "assertiveness
training," or "getting yours," or "being your own best friend"
is a book about the "soul of selling." And selling, when it's
stripped to its *soul,* involves both the knowledge and appreciation of a product, and the knowledge and appreciation of
yourself.

If a housewife receives an expensive delivery of meat and
discovers that it has the same consistency as a very expensive
piece of leather, a book on assertiveness training might help
her recognize her right to bring the meat back to the butcher
and get a refund. A good sales background will result in the
same sort of assertive behavior, but in addition it will equip
the housewife with a keener insight into the transaction.

Most interpersonal interactions can relate directly to a
sales interaction. They all ultimately involve a set of needs or
expectations, and the fulfillment of those needs. Women who
are most successful in sales learn to respect both sides of an
interaction and to anticipate all sorts of problems.

Consider a college graduate who applies for her first job.

In order to impress a potential employer she has to appreciate and convey her own worth. The very same sense of self-worth and articulation comes into play each time a young saleswoman presents herself to a new client.

Selling to others can be a strikingly effective way to learn about yourself and how the world sees you. Even if you ultimately decide to move in another career direction, the poise, confidence and valuable sense of your own worth that evolve naturally from a year or two in the sales arena are qualities that you'll carry with you.

CHAPTER

4

Women's Work

Janet Boswell sells life insurance for Equitable and is currently earning more than $40,000 a year. When she began selling she was overwhelmed by the amount of information she had to digest. Knowing what you're talking about in the insurance business can be quite a chore. But unlike her male counterparts, Janet had no trouble initiating sales and developing a client list. The hardest part of any entry-level sales job is getting appointments, and women have a built-in edge when it comes to making contacts. "A male businessman has been called on so often by male agents," Janet explained, "that when they hear a woman calling they're more apt to give an interview out of curiosity, out of 'Can *she* know what *she's* talking about?' "

Alayne Kandell sells pharmaceuticals for an international corporation. She points out that there are advantages and disadvantages to being a woman in sales. A disadvantage is that men don't have much confidence in what a woman knows when it comes to something as technical as medication. "But," she says emphatically, "right off, a woman has about a five-minute advantage over any man. Most of the men I deal with are more interested in speaking with a woman than they are with a man."

Judy Richter is fifty-three years old and vice-president of a company that imports electronic components and sells them to manufacturers of appliances. All of the engineers she deals with are men, and despite the hurdle, "What can a woman know about electronics?" she thinks that the very fact of her gender works more to her advantage than her disadvantage. "Doors are open to me with presidents of companies where my boss could not get in. They're all very, very curious to see Judy Richter, Vice-President, selling electronic components."

Most prospective buyers are men, and most men prefer to see women. Whether their motivation in wanting to see women has to do with idle curiosity, sexual curiosity, or a break in the monotony of their routine, the result of their interest is that women have an easier time getting appointments than men. Women in sales are no longer unique, but they are still unusual, and buyers are still curious to see what a sales-*woman* looks and sounds like.

Of course this ease in getting appointments is no guarantee of a sale. There are other hurdles to leap. But making initial contact is a good solid beginning, and a three-minute edge over a man is better than no edge at all. It gives you three minutes to deal with the "misimpression" that a woman selling pharmaceuticals/insurance/electronic components can't possibly know what she's talking about.

Tackling the Myths

People who don't understand sales have very strong negative feelings about it, and one man's opinion isn't always powerful enough to break through the bad mythology. Once women begin working in sales positions they begin to understand what I'm talking about, and now that so many women have succeeded in sales some of the stigma has been lifted. But there's no getting around the fact that sales has a bad reputation. Sue Salko (the saleswoman for Western Union you read about earlier) had a totally irrational idea that all salesmen were sleazy and dishonest—even though her own father was a salesman and he wasn't at all sleazy and dishonest. Why did it take her so long to let go of the sales stigma?

Recently I set up the Careers For Women Los Angeles office. One of the women at the initial meeting waited for me after the lecture and told me that her father was president of a major insurance company. She spoke about her childhood, when her father was a salesman with the same company, and how they'd always been "well off." She grew up in a big house with a swimming pool in the backyard, live-in help, and pretty much whatever she wanted. She went on to say that recently her father has been trying to persuade her to get into sales. Part of what he told her was that she could make a very, very comfortable living selling insurance, and that sales was an ideal springboard into management.

Still, she had a very negative image of sales. She never connected her comfortable upbringing with the fact that her father was a salesman. Oddly enough, until she heard my initial lecture she'd "pooh-poohed" all of her father's advice. Once she actually stopped to think about it all, her father's advice took on new meaning. What better proof did she need? Her father had been a salesman: her family had always been financially secure. Her father had been a salesman: he was currently the president of his company. Why did it take her so long to let go of the sales stigma?

A host of women that I've met through Careers For Women have needed to be virtually hit over the head with $30,000 before they would allow themselves a great career opportunity. Part of their difficulty in letting go of a negative sales image involves letting go of a feminine role. Remember those "women's jobs" I discussed earlier, all of which are extensions of a woman's role in the home, and all of which are attached to low salaries. Before a woman can allow herself to enjoy the business world she has to believe that it isn't her sole responsibility to teach children, or to be of assistance to men, or to feed the public. In essence, before women can take care of themselves they have to believe that they don't bear the burden of self-sacrifice.

The specific problem that women have with sales involves the "misimpression" I described earlier. There may be a historical basis for that misimpression (the itinerant salesman that we all met in *The Music Man* wasn't a very inspiring role-model) but it's important to keep history in its place—the past. If you were to apply the fast-talking techniques of Harold Hill to today's business world you would have little more than Trouble, with a capital "T" that rhymes with "P" that stands for Poor!

The best way to deal with the sales stigma is to approach it head-on. Let's examine the myths about sales and then replace those myths with some hard-hitting reality.

Salesmen Are Dishonest

Some salesmen may be dishonest. Usually there's a direct correlation between how successful a salesman is and how honest he is. The kind of sales jobs you're about to explore simply don't tolerate a slippery "technique." Executive sales representatives usually deal with the same people over a period of years. You can't get a signature on the bottom of a contract that doesn't deliver and expect the same person to do business with you next year. Successful salespeople need to build a clientele, and it's to their advantage to build relationships of trust.

Salesmen Have to Live on Commission

At Careers For Women I never recommend that women take straight commission sales positions. Such positions do exist, but not with most major companies. In the first place, who needs the insecurity of not having a regular paycheck? Since I appreciate that women work because they need the money, I couldn't, in good conscience, recommend a job with no salary. But more important than the insecurity of a commission-only job is the fact that nearly all good sales jobs pay a guaranteed salary. Often the salary will be between $10,000 and $15,000 a year, but that salary is only an earnings base. Most of the jobs in which I place women pay a base salary *plus* a commission. There's no reason for anyone to work on a straight commission basis.

Salesmen Are Always on the Road

There are as many different kinds of sales jobs as there are different kinds of industries. *Some* salesmen are on the road a great deal. But even those salesmen who spend time on the road have different definitions of "on the road." A pharmaceutical sales representative does most of her selling from a car, but her sales territory can be her own neighborhood. And many sales positions require no travel at all, other than the area's best restaurant. As I discuss each industry I'll be more specific about travel requirements. There are enough exciting sales positions that require limited travel (or no travel at all) so that you can pick and choose.

Salesmen Need to Be Aggressive

Alice Cummings, the electronic components saleswoman, had learned that in her business being aggressive can be fatal. In most sophisticated business environments the "big push" just won't work. People simply don't like to be pressured. If you can explain to them why they need your product, then they'll buy it. But it's to your advantage to let them make the final decision. Successful sales representatives aren't aggressive, but they *are* persistent and persuasive.

Salesmen Have to Deal with Constant Rejection

The issue of "rejection" in sales is a very important one. Part of dealing with having people say "no" to you requires that you don't personalize. A woman selling office machines for Pitney Bowes put it very clearly: "Just because someone doesn't want to buy my copier doesn't mean they don't like me!"

Consider the difference between "rejection" and "disappointment." If I were at a discotheque and I asked a woman to dance I would hope that she'd accept. If she didn't accept I'd feel *disappointed,* but I'd go on to ask someone else. If the second and third women declined my invitation I'd feel very disappointed, and if nearly every woman in the room refused to dance with me I'd feel rejected. At some point my thinking would shift from "She may not feel like dancing" to "What am I doing wrong?"

Imagine how differently I'd feel, however, if I were approaching women and asking them if they'd care to dance with my friend (at the table over there in the corner). I can assure you that my personal feelings wouldn't even enter into the picture if a roomful of women chose not to dance with my friend—even if he were a *very* good friend.

Selling is like asking someone to dance with your friend!

The Sales Personality

Of course, not all people—not even all women—are suited for a successful career in sales. There *is* such a thing as a "sales personality," and most successful sales representatives have a strong mix of all the "sales personality-components." Some of you may be particularly strong in one area and thus compensate for a weakness in another, but all of you who have real potential in sales will have a strong mix of similar character traits. Once all of the negative myths of a sales personality have been dispelled we're left with six essential *ingredients*. They are: a pleasant appearance, intelligence, verbal skills, a pleasing disposition, good character, and strong motivation. Let's examine these sales attributes more closely.

Appearance

Looking good does not mean being "beautiful" as defined by Hugh Hefner. More important than being traditionally pretty is that you project an image appropriate to your environment and your product. If you want to be taken seriously you have to look like someone who should be taken seriously.

The maître d' at an expensive restaurant isn't likely to usher you toward a good table if you're cracking gum and batting three-inch eyelashes. People aren't going to want to get close to you if you have greasy hair and perspiration stains on your blouse. A handshake is less appealing if your nails are bitten to the quick.

Of course, the appropriate look may vary from industry to industry. One pharmaceutical firm advises its sales representatives to dress like bankers—not like doctors. Doctors, they say, don't dress very well, and most doctors tend to trust the appearance of their bankers. We'll get more specific about each industry later, but for now it's enough to understand that appearance establishes a first impression, and that a good first impression is very important in sales.

Intelligence

While you needn't have the *kind* of intelligence to design a temperature control system for Honeywell, if you're the woman selling that system you need the intelligence to understand it. If you keep in mind that the best *selling* is *explaining,* you'll understand that every good saleswoman must have an in-depth knowledge of her product and of the competition. Your appearance will help you get into an office, but your intelligence is what keeps you there and gets you invited back.

Women in sales don't make their living by looking good. They have to know what they're talking about. Most companies have intensive product education, so you don't need to start out with a knowledge of chemistry, for example, to sell pharmaceuticals. But you must have the kind of intelligence that will make your "product orientation" possible. Different kinds of intelligence, of course, are required to sell different kinds of products. If you flunked high school chemistry you probably shouldn't anticipate a brilliant career selling for Squibb, but there's no reason for you to be anything less than brilliant selling advertising space.

Verbal Skills

Verbal skills are really an extension of "intelligence." Potential buyers aren't mind readers. You might have extensive knowledge of your product, but if you can't communicate what you know, you're not going to make sales.

But knowing how to communicate verbally doesn't mean that you need to be a great orator. You need only feel comfortable with conversation. Often too impassioned a sales pitch can turn clients off, or make them feel like they're being pushed. Remember, a good salesperson is never pushy!

Disposition

Like appearance, a pleasing disposition is crucial to making a good first impression. In a word, no one eagerly anticipates dealing with a chronically depressed, angry, self-righteous, complaining or whining person. If you're going to succeed in sales you have to be likable. And there's no way to fake that quality.

When you sell, you want your clients to like you. They should feel good when they note your lunch date on their calendar, and they should anticipate your meeting as a pleasant break from the routine of their day. Consider the saleswoman I discussed earlier who noticed that her client was interested in gourmet cooking. There's no question that her client will eagerly anticipate their next meeting.

If you don't enjoy meeting people, you won't like sales. But you needn't be overly outgoing, and you'll be damned if you're too aggressive.

Character

Good character supports good disposition the way intelligence supports a good appearance. Successful saleswomen are honest and frank, and it is these qualities that insure solid, long-term business relationships. If you sell someone something he doesn't need, he's not going to think kindly of you when he discovers exactly what it is that he does need. If you promise results that don't happen, you'll lose all of your credibility. A charming disposition may get you *one* deal, but one *shady* deal can ruin a career.

Motivation

All successful people, in all walks of life, understand the importance of motivation. And sales is no exception. To be successful you must be persistent and willing to work hard. You need to set short- and long-term goals and work toward accomplishing them. "Motivation" is the energy force that connects all five of the other "sales personality" ingredients. If your energy level is low, it will reflect in your career.

Strong motivation is particularly important in sales. Although sales executives don't have to worry about getting doors slammed in their faces, they often hear potential clients say, "No, I don't think that's what we're looking for." A successful saleswoman must have the motivation to see her through several such negative responses. You need the persistence to pick up the receiver and try again, and again, and again—if necessary. And you need the confidence to understand that a negative response is not a personal rejection. Eventually your effort will pay off. We'll discuss the facts of "sales and rejection" later, but for now you have to consider whether or not you're a highly motivated person.

Would You Be a Successful Saleswoman?

The following questions are designed to help you discover whether or not you have a natural bent toward sales. I'd suggest that you get a paper and pencil and make an attempt to *write* your answers down. Think about what you're saying and how honest you're being with yourself. The point of your answers isn't to get 100 percent. Rather, you should use this little quiz as a diagnostic tool.

The answers that I've provided are more than answers.

They're designed to illustrate the point of each question and how it relates to a particular character trait that will help you in your new career. Compare the answers you've written with my answers and analyze them for similarities. I'm much more interested in *tone* here than I am in "yes" and "no."

1. Do you have a financial need to work?

2. Do you have an ego need to work?

3. Do you enjoy participating in sports?

4. Do you like to play games? (Cards, Scrabble, charades, etc.)

5. How do you feel when you lose, beyond good or bad?

6. Do you prefer to watch an activity, or to engage in it? Why?

7. How would someone who's known you for a long time but who doesn't like you describe you?

8. Describe a social situation in which you feel very comfortable.

9. When you're faced with a frightening situation, or a situation in which you don't perform well, do you tend to back out?

10. At what point in your life were you the most popular with your peer group? What do you owe that popularity to?

11. Do people tend to confide in you or ask you for advice?

12. If someone didn't like you at first sight, what would be their objections?

13. If you go to the movies with friends do you often end up seeing something *you* really didn't want to see?

14. Do you feel that you can "visit" on the telephone?

15. What is the most significant accomplishment up to this point in your life?

1. Think back to what I discussed earlier about motivation. It's important to be serious about entering a new career.

Financial need can be a very strong motivation. If your rent is due at the beginning of each month, and if you're the one who's going to have to pay it, it's much more likely that you'll work hard to insure the income than if you were living off a trust fund that your great-grandfather established in your name. You can define "need" however you want. It may be that you want to buy something terribly extravagant and that despite the fact that your husband makes a good living you won't be able to indulge yourself unless you pitch in. If that's the case, you should count yourself among those who have a financial need to work. Needing money may make life harder, but it makes success much more visible.

2. An ego need to work can be just as important as a financial need to work. It's best, of course, if you have both an ego need and a financial need to work. The more you *need* to work—whatever your reasons—the harder you're likely to work. But "ego need" is very important, and these days it's particularly important for women. It's important for all people to be able to see themselves as a success. The fact is that in our society success (as well as power) is defined by money. You're more likely to feel successful if you're earning a "successful person's income." That sort of drive is important to a sales career.

3 & 4. There's a lot implied by these two questions. First of all, people who like to participate in sports or games usually enjoy competition, and people who enjoy competition generally have a good deal of self-confidence. Self-confidence is important in sales. Confident people usually convey their sense of "self" when they interact, and in a sales situation an attitude of "self-confidence" can actually create an *atmosphere* of trust and confidence. Second, people who participate in sports or games generally enjoy contact with other people. Both sports and games require a high degree of sociability and a good saleswoman *must* enjoy people.

5. No one, other than a masochist, enjoys losing. A suc-

cessful saleswoman should hate to lose. But what exactly does *hating to lose* mean? If every time you lose you begin to question your own worth, then you'd best not get involved in sales. But if you use your own failures to insure future success—if you examine what you did wrong, what you might have done better, and what you can do that will enhance your performance—then you're very well suited for sales. Ideally you should meet a failure with an eagerness to try again.

6. The best salespeople are what I call "activists." If you like to *do* things more than you like to watch other people do things, then you're likely to do well in sales. "Doers" tend to have confidence in themselves and be willing to try things without the fear of "losing face." An "activist" personality usually enjoys watching other people do things only as preparation for diving in themselves.

7. Hopefully you'll have a harder time answering this question, but some thought should produce a few answers. People in sales shouldn't always be burdened with their worst personality traits, but it's important to be honest enough with yourself to improve on your flaws. If the flaws that you've listed here included "dishonest, manipulative, can't be trusted," then you may have problems in sales. If you've listed such things as "too persistent, self-important, too fussy," then you can work on those problems and turn them into sales strengths.

8. If you've described a social situation in which you are very passive, then you may have some problems in sales. If you described a situation in which you're with a group of good friends and participating in some group activity, then you're in good shape. The implication is that you *have* a group of good friends (no, everyone doesn't have a group of good friends, but it's a good sign that you asked). You're in still better shape if you described a social activity that involves meeting new people. If you loathe the idea of meeting people you'll have some problems in sales. If you love the idea of new

people and new situations you're probably a born saleswoman.

9. Once again, this question involves self-image. Ideally, a salesperson should forge ahead in uncomfortable situations. Everyone is frightened by new situations, and everyone performs less well in some situations than in others, but successful people don't let their fear cripple them. One woman I met actually created a litany of "I can do this I can do this I can do this." It may sound corny, but it worked for her. I'm not suggesting that you "Whistle a Happy Tune," but you have to develop a method for overcoming fear. If you tend to throw your hands up in the air and quit, you'll have problems. Think about your past. How have you dealt with problems that arose from marriage, child-rearing, college? You may have more gumption than you give yourself credit for.

10. You should have some sense of identification with this question. You needn't have been the high-school prom queen to consider yourself popular, but "popularity" suggests that people find you likable. If you recall, likability is an important quality for a saleswoman. It's also important that you don't reach too far back in history when you think of your most popular period. Ideally your answer should be "Now." If you're thirty-five years old and have declared your pre-teen years to be your most popular, then you're probably somewhat stuck in the past. Being stuck in the past doesn't promise much success for the future. If you answered the second part of this question by describing a set of circumstances (e.g., I was in a good sorority, I had great clothing, etc.), then you've missed the point. Ideally the things that account for your popularity should have to do with things *you've* initiated (e.g., *I* made a real effort to meet people, *I* enjoyed doing things for people, even if they were a little inconvenient, etc.).

11. If people tend to confide in you or ask you for advice it means that you present yourself as someone worthy of trust. That trait is crucial to a successful sales career. If you can be trusted with someone's secrets—if people allow them-

selves to be vulnerable in front of you—then they're likely to trust your advice with regard to their business needs as well.

12. This question should have you stumped. Unlike Question No. 7, I'm not talking here about a person who's had time to get to know you. If you have a reasonably good self-image you should have a hard time thinking of qualities a perfect stranger would pick out in a first meeting. If you have a long list of such qualities (I'm too fat, I talk too much, my hair is bad, etc.), then you've got your work cut out for you. First impressions are crucial for business contacts. They give you entree and pave the way for second impressions, and third impressions, and successful closings.

13. A key to sales success is the ability to persuade. If you find that you are always being *persuaded* rather than being the person who *does* the persuading, then you may not be a good sales personality. If you never go to movies, apply the question of "persuasion" to another situation. If you're with some friends and trying to decide where to go for dinner, are people usually excited by your suggestions? Do your children usually go along with your plans because you've made them sound exciting, or do you have to drag them along against their will? When you make a great discovery (a new shop, a new show, a new recipe, a new business opportunity), can you convey your enthusiasm in such a way that the person you're talking to begins to feel as excited as you do?

14. In many areas of sales, telephone work is crucial. Frequently a saleswoman will make her first approach—her request for an appointment—over the phone. In order to be successful in that approach you need to feel comfortable with the telephone. You can judge whether or not you have "phone ability" by examining your use of the phone in your personal life. People who tense up on the telephone tend to sound entirely different when they make a call than they do in person. People who are comfortable with the telephone can create the illusion of a visit, can actually make you forget that you're

talking over an instrument. There are certain "phone techniques" that we'll discuss later which may help you make initial contact, but most important is your ability to make *real* contact even when you're talking into a receiver.

15. The most important thing about how you answered this last question isn't so much *what* you listed as your accomplishment but *how* you described your role in bringing it about. If, for example, you said, "My most significant accomplishment to date has been the birth of my three children," then you're actually describing something that happened *to* you, rather than saying, "My most significant accomplishment to date has been raising three children and creating an open and loving home environment for them to grow in." Even if both of those women have been doing the same thing for the last ten years, the *way* in which they described themselves suggests that they see themselves quite differently. Whatever you've indicated here as your most significant accomplishment to date, read your answer carefully and see to what extent you've included yourself. Have you described things as happening *to* you, or have you described events that you've initiated? As you become involved in sales you'll learn to appreciate the importance of self-motivation. If you see yourself as a "doer" you won't have any problem.

Now that you've answered each question and read my answers to each question you should have some sense of where your natural sales strengths are, and where your weaknesses lie. As I said earlier, a natural sales talent needn't be strong in all aspects of what I've identified as "the sales personality." You may have discovered that you're outstandingly motivated but that you just don't make a very good appearance. All of your talent may lie in your verbal ability and intelligence, but you may need to get your act together with regard to your disposition. The important thing is that you have a strong mix of the qualities I've discussed. You can work on areas that you think may need improvement, and you can ask friends for feedback. Finally, you have to accept yourself—with your weaknesses and with your strengths—and take the plunge. The water may be a bit cold at first, but your body will make the adjustment. The most successful saleswomen haven't measured themselves against any outside image or standard. They've relied on their natural ability to float and have learned the most effective strokes and kicks after they spent some time in the water.

You Can If You Want To

Now that I've given you some sense of what I think is important in a saleswoman, I want to tell you a story that illustrates how wrong I can be. I don't enjoy being on public display with egg on my face, but there's an important lesson in my mistake: there are no rules.

When I first began Careers For Women I used a selective process in determining who would take my courses. I didn't have the kind of staff that I have today, and I felt confident that I could pick the women with the greatest potential. Since the first few years of any business venture are usually pretty rough, and since I was only paid by companies after I placed a woman successfully (I offer a six-month money-back guarantee to all of the companies with whom I place saleswomen), I didn't feel that I could gamble on a roomful of women that I didn't think had what it takes.

After I had been in business for a few months a woman named Rochelle came to interview for the course. She was overweight, somewhat retiring, not at all well dressed, and she had a very strong New York accent. She told me that she had never made more than $8,500 a year, that she was thirty-three years old and that she had heard about me from a friend. She wasn't like the Diane Coles that I'd hired in the past, and she was nothing like the other women who had been participating in my program. I told her, quite frankly, that I didn't see her in sales. (And I told her, not as frankly, that I was sure she'd be successful at something else.) She pleaded with me to let her attend a few lectures but I stood firm. She said she was certain that she'd be a good saleswoman, but again I stood firm.

The rest of this story may sound incredible to you, and it was, in fact, incredible. One evening in April I left my building shortly after my lecture. It was raining out and Rochelle was standing, with an umbrella, in front of my building. "Look," she said, "I don't know what I have to do to convince you that I'm going to be good in sales, but I've been standing here in the rain for the last hour trying to get up my nerve to ask you just one more time to let me take your course. I *know* that I've got what you're looking for!"

You may recall that *persistence* was one of the qualities that I considered to be crucial to a successful sales career. Rochelle may have been a total zero with regard to everything else, but I don't think I've ever met a more patient and persistent woman. So I said she could come to the next class.

She went through the entire program and, finally, I wasn't able to place her in a sales job. As far as I could tell, my talent for picking winners (and losers) had been confirmed. Nearly four years after she left Careers For Women I bumped into her in front of a restaurant in New York. She turned to the colleague with her and introduced me as "the man who changed my life." She called me the next day to fill me in on what had happened to her since she left my classroom. Apparently she spent a few years looking for her niche, but found it two years ago. She was currently a sales representative for a chemical company. She wasn't quite certain of how much she was earning this year but last year she filed for $28,000.

Our conversation ended with her telling me that her company was very interested in hiring more saleswomen and that she was certain her sales manager would be interested in talking with me. Rochelle had given me a client and (unwittingly) changed my entire mode of operation. I *never* turn down a woman who wants to take the Careers For Women program. I've come to realize that no one knows better than you do whether you've got what it takes to be successful in sales. If you think you can sell, and if you want to sell, then you'll sell!

PART

2

How to Get There

5

Selecting a Career Path in Sales

Job vs. Career

Sales has always been a springboard into management. Most of the men who enter corporations through the sales door don't plan on staying there for very long. There's no reason why sales shouldn't serve the same function for women. Once you learn to distinguish between a *job* and a *career* there won't be any limit on where you can go.

Kathy Aaronson, who works with Careers For Women, began her career by selling advertising space. She was one of the first women to sell advertising space for *Cosmopolitan* magazine, and she was the first person to convince manufacturers of typewriters that it would pay for them to run ads in women's magazines. Her logic was that it was a secretary who used a typewriter, and when it came time to order new machines most executives would ask their secretaries how they felt about the machine they were using.

She had a series of jobs after she left *Cosmo*. At one point she was the Advertising Manager of *"W,"* a very exclusive women's publication. Finally she was made Vice-President, Editorial Chairman, and Publisher at McFadden Publications.

The important thing for you to glean from Kathy's success is that she always had her eye on "the next step." There's absolutely no limit on where you may end up.

Most women make job decisions. When you make a job decision you ask yourself questions. What kind of work am I going to be doing? How much am I going to be paid? Who are the people I'm going to be surrounded by?

I don't think those are the right questions to ask. I don't want to help you make *job* decisions. Rather, I want women to learn to think in terms of *career* decisions. There's a big difference. When you think *career,* you think long-term. You ask yourself questions like: If I do this very well, how much will I be earning in a year? in two years? in five years? What are my promotional opportunities? Where do *I* want to be in five years and what am I willing to put up with in order to get there? You can "fall into" a job, but you can't "fall into" a career.

Consider a woman who says to herself, "I'm very underpaid but my boss is nice and I'm happy on a day-to-day basis." There's a lot implied in that kind of thinking. Implication number one is that she should be grateful that her boss is pleasant and that there's something precarious about that circumstance. If she went somewhere else her boss might not be so nice. In short, she feels *lucky* to be treated well.

In fact, it's entirely likely that this woman's boss treats her *nicely* because he values her, as would anyone else she worked for. And, if you'll excuse what appears to be a truism, they value her because she *is* valuable.

Implication number two of that woman's thinking is that

she should accept being underpaid because it's part of a trade-off: being treated well requires that she be underpaid. That sort of thinking doesn't hold up once you've entered the real world of women in business. As soon as this woman finds out that someone else is making twice her salary in addition to enjoying her environment, the floor will fall out of the reasoning behind her trade-off. Who ever said that you needed to sacrifice salary for satisfaction?

There's a lot you need to get wise to if you're seriously planning a career. I recently sat on a panel discussion with Betty Harragan. Ms. Harragan wrote a book called *Games Mother Never Taught You: Corporate Gamesmanship for Women*. When she spoke about promotions she made a very important distinction between promotions into *line* jobs and promotions into *staff* jobs.

As much as I dislike generalities about the business world, her point is an important one. Staff jobs have traditionally been open to women, and they're not nearly as desirable as the jobs traditionally closed to women. Staff jobs are the kinds of jobs that support, supply and feed the line jobs. Line jobs are where all of the decisions get made.

"Staff departments make up a separate part of the company," Ms. Harragan says. "They are not profit centers, they are expenses. However vital their services, they cost the company money to operate, and in an economic recession staff jobs are the first ones cut. Thus, staff jobs are not training grounds for future policy-making officers of the corporation. Staff vice-presidents have authority *only* over the people in their department; they report to a line vice-president who is their superior. A staff executive is never empowered to make *policy* decisions; those are the prerogatives of line executives."

Try to figure out what a staff position might be. If you're thinking of advertising, public relations, personnel, and accounting, you're thinking right. Try to avoid a promotion from sales into a *staff* job. As soon as you stop bringing money *into* the company and start *costing* the company money, you become expendable.

When you begin to ask *career* questions, you develop a whole new set of priorities. If you're interested in becoming a district sales manager in five years, and one of the best ways to reach that goal involves working under a particularly unpleasant man for six months, you may decide to put up with his unpleasantness. What does six months mean in terms of a career?

Judy Boston wanted to sell advertising space. She had several degrees and over ten years' experience in teaching, but she wanted to make a career change and she wanted to make money. After she left Careers For Women she couldn't get a job on a magazine. Everywhere she went she was told that they needed people with experience. Finally, in desperation, she accepted a straight commission job selling advertising space for a local Yellow Pages.

She worked harder than she had ever worked in her life. There was nothing glamorous about her job, and she made very little money. But she was very future-oriented and stuck with it for six months. Then she began looking for a good job again. When asked if she had experience she said, "Yes," and after a month of job hunting she accepted a job with an important New York newspaper, *The Village Voice*.

The six-month sacrifice was clearly worth it in view of her new job and life-style. She has a guaranteed salary, an expense account, and the prestige of a good publication. When and if she decides to move on she'll have no problem moving up the ladder.

Faye Whitfield Prout was in the second sales training program given by Careers For Women in 1973. She had graduated cum laude from Lincoln University in Pennsylvania, with a B.A. in liberal arts, just two years before she began our program. When she came to us, Faye had worked for

Guidance Associates (a subsidiary of Harcourt Brace Jovanovich) as a project editor from January 1972 to March 1973 when she was promoted to Assistant Director of the Educational Film Division.

In April 1974 we placed her with Merrill Lynch as an account executive. Her salary there was $12,000 plus commissions, and in 1975 she was the only black female account executive among five thousand brokers.

In September 1976 she left Merrill Lynch to become a registered representative in retail sales for Lehman Brothers Kuhn Loeb, Inc. And after two years on the job she was promoted to Vice-President, Lehman Securities. Today, at twenty-seven, Faye earns above the $50,000 benchmark most often used to identify top executives.

Not all women follow the same success path as Faye Whitfield Prout or Judy Boston. But there is a fairly well trod path from sales into management. A typical career path in a Fortune 500 company might be as follows:

1. Saleswoman, entry-level trainee for six months to a year.

2. Area Sales Representative for a year. One out of three moves on to—

3. Key Accounts or National Accounts Representative for one year. One out of every four moves on to—

4. Assistant Manager for one to two years. One out of four moves on to—

5. District Manager for one to five years

6. Regional Manager for one to five years

7. General Sales Manager or National Sales Manager

8. Vice-President, Marketing, or Vice-President, Sales

9. President

In a smaller company the path into management may be somewhat different. Usually, tradition indicates this sort of career movement:

1. Sales Representative
2. Sales Manager
3. Vice-President, Sales
4. Equity position (stock or partnership)
5. President

Now that you're beginning to think in terms of *career,* it's time to get specific about sales. Sales is not one career. There are as many different careers in sales as there are industries, and there are many sales jobs outside of the major industries; it's important in starting out to select the right career path in sales.

Certain industries will afford you the opportunity to move very quickly. Others will be long-term growth industries. There are some areas in sales that have very defined limits.

I've developed eighteen evaluative criteria which can be applied to every area of sales. The questions these criteria address themselves to will help you determine where a particular industry will lead. Before you enter an industry, you should have an idea about where that industry can take you.

But given all the information, your final decision will always be subjective. What will make you happy? Are you bent on rising in the corporation? Do you think you'll be happy remaining in sales? What kind of sales atmosphere suits *you* best? It's important to make your subjective decisions on the basis of information—not on the basis of ignorance.

The Criteria

Let's begin by studying these criteria in the abstract. After I discuss the criteria generally, I'll apply them to the specific industries and you'll be able to make some informed decisions.

Money

I want to start talking about money because money is important in sales and in everything else. Starting remuneration in sales will come in one of four forms: straight commission, flat salary, guaranteed salary plus commission/bonus, or draw-advance against commission.

The first payment structure—*straight commission*—is the least popular and, therefore, least common. It's least popular because it doesn't offer financial security or cash flow, and it's least common because those companies that are looking for straight commission people are in competition with companies that offer more attractive modes of remuneration. The people who apply for straight commission jobs are usually the bottom of the sales barrel—the ones who can't do any better. If you had a choice between a straight commission job with expected earnings of $15,000, or a guaranteed salary of $15,000, you'd have to be pretty dim to say, "I want to take a chance and go on straight commission."

The second least desirable payment structure is a *flat salary*. Flat salary is not too popular because salespeople look to something beyond a good salary for motivation. Motivation means incentive, and in sales, incentive means that your salary will *directly* reflect your work. The less abstract the relationship between your income and your performance, the better for you. If you've done well and haven't gotten a raise, it's a good feeling to be able to quote your sales volume as evidence of your performance. But it's a better feeling to not have to ask for a raise at all.

Which brings us to the third form of remuneration: *guaranteed salary plus bonus,* or *guaranteed salary plus commission*. Let's start with salary plus commission.

If your salary is $15,000 and there's a high predictability of your selling $100,000 worth of supplies or services, how would I, as an employer, give you an incentive? First, I'd calculate that if you met my $100,000 projection I could afford for you to earn an extra $3,000 a year above your salary. (All of these figures are for the sake of example.) Three thousand dollars is 3 percent of $100,000, so I'd tell you that in addition to your salary I'd be prepared to give you 3 percent of everything that you sold. By the time you sold the anticipated $100,000, your income will have reached $18,000 and both you (the saleswoman) and I (the employer) will be ahead of the game.

At that point the best thing that could happen for us both would be for you to sell beyond the $100,000 prediction. If you went on to sell $200,000 then I'd be well ahead of my $100,000 goal, and your 3 percent commission would total $6,000. This mode of payment is ideal in situations where an employer has a clear idea of what he can expect, and a clear means of measuring the output of each individual sales representative. But such isn't always the case.

It could be that you're trying a new product in a new area. If I, as an employer, had no idea of what I could reasonably expect from you, I'd have no way to figure out a commission percentage. Or suppose that you were part of a sales team and it were difficult to separate the performance of one member of the team from the others. Given either of these two situations I still have to figure out a way to give you an incentive above salary. In such instances some corporations will offer a bonus rather than a percentage. An employer may say, "I'll pay you a salary of $15,000 a year plus a bonus of not less than $3,000 (or a *discretionary bonus*) at the end of your first year." If by the end of that year you've done well, your bonus will reflect your success. If the new territory you're pioneering doesn't pan out, you'll still get a bonus. Your employer will get a set of figures from which to calculate his projections for the following year.

The fourth form of remuneration is known as *draw against commission* or *advance against commission*. The words *draw* and *advance* are used interchangeably. There are two kinds of draw against commission situations. The first is called *recriminatory draw*. Recriminatory draw means that you draw $200 or $300 a week as a *loan*. An employer is literally loaning you money so that you can pay your rent and all of your living expenses until you start selling enough so that your commission equals your draw.

Assume that you are drawing annually $10,000. Your weekly draw comes to $200 against a 10 percent commission. That means that every Friday (or whenever payday is) you'll pick up a check for $200. If at the end of the year you've sold a volume of $100,000, then you break even. (Ten percent of $100,000 equals $10,000.) In a recriminatory situation if I, as your employer, advance you $200 a week and you only sell $80,000 by the end of the year, you'll owe me $2,000. And if at the end of one month you decide to quit without having made a sale, you'll owe me $800.

Sounds pretty scary, doesn't it? Well, you needn't be frightened by a recriminatory draw situation because it will never "sneak up" on you. In order for you to be hired with that sort of situation, your employer will have to get your signature on what is, in effect, a bank note which says that you'll agree to pay back the corporation. *Under no circumstances are women to ever sign a paper agreeing to a recriminatory draw arrangement*. There are too many alternatives. You don't have to "borrow" money to start your own job. It's like borrowing money to pay your own salary.

But don't be turned off by the word *draw*. One of the best ways you can get paid is the *nonrecriminatory draw*. A nonrecriminatory draw is essentially the same thing as *salary plus commission,* but it gives an employer more leeway in hiring salespeople with different experiential backgrounds. Let's use the same set of figures I used in explaining a recriminatory draw to illustrate a nonrecriminatory situation.

If you were to draw $200 a week against a 10 percent

commission and you only sold $80,000 volume by the end of the year, you'd keep your entire $10,000 annual draw, and you wouldn't owe the company anything. In the case of a non-recriminatory draw, the draw is actually a minimum guaranteed salary.

So why not just call it salary plus commission? Because a sales manager may choose to give a salesperson with more experience a bigger draw. In the long run the size of the draw won't determine total income, but it will reward experience with greater cash flow.

Consider a person who has a $12,000 draw against commission with a 10 percent commission. If that person sells $300,000 worth of material she will earn a total of $30,000. Since her draw was only $12,000, at the end of the year her company will owe her $18,000. If another salesperson has been hired for a draw of $25,000 and sells the same $300,000 worth of material she'll still earn $30,000 that year. Her company, however, will only owe her $5,000 at the end of the year. Since the situation is nonrecriminatory—which means you never have to pay back the company for what you don't sell—you're obviously at an advantage in terms of personal cash flow if you have a bigger draw.

The specific arrangement of the draw may be somewhat complicated. They may say that they'll give you no commission on the first $65,000 because they regard that as your *quota*. Your commission above that $65,000 will be 2¼ percent on your first $200,000, 1¼ percent up to $300,000, ½ percent up to $400,000, and so on. All of these fractions add up to something very concrete, and it's that total that you should be concerned with. Don't ever be intimidated by what appears to be a complicated commission arrangement.

Some women think that the draw *against* commission—even though it's nonrecriminatory—implies a psychological disadvantage. They may be concerned that if their earnings come to $3,000 less than their draw, their company will *think* of them as being $3,000 in debt. In fact, they're no more in debt than a saleswoman who has earned a $3,000 salary but not made enough sales to cover her salary.

There is a situation called *carry-over-minus* that deals specifically with the above circumstance. In a carry-over-minus arrangement, if your earnings are $3,000 short of your draw you'll go into the new year with a "minus $3,000." This "minus" figure is usually theoretical. It exists mainly on paper and means little in terms of your income. For most sales managers will say, "Look, there was a problem with your territory and we're going to wipe out that $3,000 and begin the new year with a clean slate."

Remember that unless you've signed a paper stating otherwise, there should be no obligation whatsoever on your part in a *draw against commission* system of remuneration. If the word *draw* makes you tense, then replace it in your mind with the word *salary*.

The most important thing that women in sales need to understand about money is that during an interview you must exhibit as much interest in the potential commissions as you do in the guaranteed salary. We'll discuss what to do on an interview in more detail later, but keep in mind that if you press the issue of guaranteed salary an employer will tend to think that you don't plan to do much selling.

Starting Benefits

The important thing when evaluating benefits is to try to attach a cash value to each specific benefit. Once you've finished this kind of an evaluation you can add up the cash values and increase your projected earnings by their total. If you expect to earn $25,000 but the benefits of the job add up to another $7,000, then you should think of yourself in terms

of earning $32,000. If you're offered another job with pro-
jected earnings of $30,000 but no benefits, you'd be earning
$2,000 less. Let's consider some of the most common benefits.

Many sales positions offer an *automobile*. Auto benefits
usually mean that the company buys you a $6,000 car, pays
for your insurance, maintenance, upkeep and gas, and gives
you the freedom to use the car as though it were your own. A
car should be figured into your earnings at $2,500 a year *tax
free*. (The company pays all taxes on its automobiles.)

Health and medical plans vary from company to company. You can determine what your health and medical benefits are worth by calling up Blue Cross/Blue Shield and telling
them that you're interested in the cost of the following kind of
health plan—then describe the plan that your company is
offering. Whatever they tell you the cost of that plan is will
be the value of your health and medical benefits.

Dental plans are never available to individuals—only to
corporations. Therefore if you want to weigh the value of a
dental plan you'll need to take a look at your dental bills over
the last five years and average them. Your average annual cost
of dental care is likely to be what the dental benefits are worth
to you. Of course, it's possible that you've been putting off a
lot of root canal work because you didn't have the money. If
that's the case, then dental benefits could be worth a great deal
more to you.

Pension plans shouldn't be considered unless you're on
the mature side of forty. In sales there's a great deal of movement. It's unlikely that a twenty-eight-year-old woman will be
in the same job at the time of her retirement. So don't be se-
duced by a great pension plan.

Profit sharing must be considered. Find out what the
average was over the last two or three years. If the average
was $200 a year, then that's about what it's worth to you.

Vacation benefits must be considered on a personal basis.
Some companies may give you four weeks' vacation a year. If

you know that you're a work-a-holic who never even takes a two-week vacation, or if your husband can't get away for four weeks and you wouldn't take a vacation without him, then the four weeks' vacation you're being offered is meaningless for you.

If, however, you love vacations and are really going to enjoy a full month, then calculate your likely four-week salary. That's what your vacation benefits will be worth.

All of the other fringe benefits can be calculated in a similar fashion. If your company is offering you a *life insurance policy,* call up Prudential (or any of the major companies) and ask them what that sort of policy would cost you. Then add that cost to the list of benefit values and tack it all onto your annual earnings.

Travel Requirements

Travel requirements have to be understood in terms of where and how often. Normally you'll want to find out about overnight travel requirements, and you should be given a percentage. A 20 percent travel requirement usually means that 20 percent of the time you'll be housed somewhere other than under your own roof. But a 20 percent travel requirement can mean different things depending on your territory.

If you're living in New York and you're told that there's a 20 percent travel requirement covering Washington, D.C., Philadelphia and Boston, you should ask whether they mean overnight travel or day travel. In the instance of a territory covering the above three cities they may say, "Well, that's up to you. If you want to, you can come back on the commuter train at night."

In addition, 20 percent travel time does not always mean the same thing in terms of your life-style. It could, for example, mean that one night out of five you'll be away from home. Or it could mean one week out of every five weeks, or two

weeks out of every ten weeks, and so on. A woman with children may have no problem getting someone to take care of
her family for one week out of every five but may find it impossible to get someone to stay overnight for two weeks out
of every ten. One night out of every week may be the easiest
arrangement of all. You need to consider every aspect of
travel time and look for an arrangement that most suits you.

You also need to understand the nature of the travel—
whether it's urban or rural travel. If you're living in New York,
travel to Chicago is fun. You'll stay in the Regency Hyatt
House. You can buy yourself a cocktail and dinner and have a
good time. But a saleswoman isn't as likely to have fun if she's
going to be traveling to small towns. When an unescorted
woman walks into a cocktail lounge in a place like Muncie,
Indiana, people look at her oddly.

Finally, you'll need to consider the mode of travel. How
do you get where you're going? If you're told that your marketing area is Chicago, Atlanta, Washington, D.C., and Boston, and there's a 20 percent travel requirement, you can reasonably conclude that you're going to be flying. If you're told
that your marketing area is upstate Pennsylvania or upstate
New York you'll probably end up driving, and driving brings
in a whole different set of problems. Among other things,
you'll have to consider how comfortable you'll be behind the
wheel for long stretches of time.

Travel and Expense Allowances

If you have a liberal travel and expense allowance, travel
can be fun. If you're only given $25 a day, you may not have
as good a time. The more liberal your corporation, the more
fun your travel is going to be.

But whatever the size of your travel allowance, it very
often requires that you have your own credit cards. Very often
a woman will apply for her first credit cards (in your own

name—not your husband's) in a job that has an expense requirement. If you don't have your own cards when you join a company they'll tell you to get them. Always get the cards in your name—not the company's name—if you're given a choice. This is your opportunity to establish a good credit rating.

Attitude Toward Women

You can't get all of the information you'll need to select a career path in sales in any one place. You obviously can't ask an interviewer what his attitude—or the attitude of his company—is toward women. If he's a rigid sexist he's not likely to say, "I hate the idea of hiring women but I'm being pressured by the federal government." You'll have to discern the attitude from several sources: social circles, annual reports, people on the sales force. If you're interested in the attitude of an entire industry you'll have to check further: read magazines, peruse the trade journals, and look for signals between the lines of what you read.

Always make a point of checking on how many women are in management positions, most importantly in line jobs. That information is important. If you have no other way of evaluating the attitude of the corporation toward women, find out the length of time the company has employed women in a certain division and check on the number of women in managerial positions within that division. It doesn't necessarily have to be sales that you investigate for it to reflect a corporate attitude.

If your research indicates that there are no women in management you'll still have a decision to make. Obviously, such industries will be more pressured legally to promote women. If you're kind of tough, you may be able to steel yourself against the negative attitude and move quickly into management. But be realistic about your sensibilities. A negative attitude toward women isn't likely to be a pleasant thing to deal with. You may have to deal with that attitude on a day-to-day, year-to-year basis.

Nature of the Selling Situation

How You Get in Front of Your Prospect

There are four ways to get in front of the prospective buyer: through leads, through prearranged appointments, through cold calling, or by servicing existing accounts. No one of these methods is objectively "the best way." Some companies used to take great pride in advertising: "We supply all of your leads." And salespeople assumed that since companies gave them leads (rather than having the salesperson call on people cold) they were offering better jobs. But you must inquire as to the nature of a company's leads. A lead means different things to different people.

At Careers For Women every week, without exception, we have three to five letters or telephone calls from prospective clients. They may say, "We've heard about you and would like more information about hiring saleswomen from you." When I give that letter to a saleswoman I'm giving her a *real* lead. I'm saying, "This is someone who's interested in finding out about us."

But if people send me their name and address in response to a full-page ad in *The New York Times* that said:

WE WILL GIVE A FREE DESK SET TO ANY SALES MANAGER
WHO RESPONDS TO THIS AD WITHIN FIVE WORK DAYS! ! !

it wouldn't be fair to consider those people to be leads. They would simply be people who wanted free desk sets. Always check out how a company defines "leads."

Prearranged appointments are the easiest and most common way to make your sales calls. You telephone someone and say, "This is my company, this is my product, this is why I think you'd be interested. Can we get together on Thursday to discuss the whole thing in detail?" When you arrive at that person's office on Thursday, he'll be expecting you and receptive enough to at least listen to what you have to say.

Cold calling (arriving without a prearranged appointment). The crucial factors in cold calling are the nature of your industry, your company's reputation, and your product. IBM, Xerox, National Cash Register, Pitney Bowes, and most other manufacturers of business equipment don't bother to prearrange appointments. They arrive at a company, give someone their business card and say, "My name is Jane Jones from National Cash Register. I'd like to see the office manager. We have something I'd like to show him."

The experience of manufacturers of office equipment has indicated that it is more costly and less efficient to try to get prearranged appointments than it is to just arrive. Most of the people they deal with are receptive to this cold calling, and in certain industries cold calling has become the tradition. If cold calling is the accepted tradition of an industry that interests you, no one will look askance at you because you just "dropped in." It helps, of course, when you're cold calling, to be with a prestigious company. The name of that company and the reputation behind it should insure you a welcome. Women have an added advantage with cold calling since prospects might respond to them in person.

If it goes against your grain to do cold calling—even in an industry where it is the established method of operation—then you have to look to other industries for your future. When you're cold calling, even though it may be the accepted practice, there's always the possibility that you will arrive at "the worst possible time." If that possibility would make you tense, then stick to an area where you'll have prearranged appointments.

Although *servicing an established account* is seemingly

the easiest way of getting contacts, it often turns out to be the most difficult. You may be hired by a company that hands you an already established account only to discover that you're inheriting a hornet's nest. Along with the inheritance of the accounts comes an inheritance of the problems. If your predecessor was irresponsible you'll reap the harvest of that irresponsibility. It could become your burden to develop a new relationship with the old people—and that can be difficult. Trust takes a long time to build up and a very short time to break down. And despite the fact that that sounds like something from a Chinese fortune cookie, the fact remains that many saleswomen who service an established account often wish they had had the opportunity to start with a clean slate.

Type of Prospect

The second thing to evaluate when you consider the nature of the selling situation is the kind of person you'll have to be selling to. You can define the type of prospect in several ways. Let's begin with gender. Men in every industry respond better to women calling on them than they do to salesmen. They usually prefer to be called upon by women. Most women also prefer to be called upon by women. (However, there are women who simply don't like other women. They feel instantly combative. If your experience shows you to be somewhat hostile toward other women, you obviously shouldn't enter an industry where you'll be calling primarily on other women.)

More important than gender, though, is your prospect's social status. Will you be calling on top management or the aisle manager of a supermarket? There are many products where you'll have to call on the top person in a company. This person is usually a very busy, hard-to-get, overbearing man. Phones will ring constantly during your presentation. He'll probably have a big office and an intimidating presence. If you're not comfortable with that, you should research other industries. If you drop down the management ladder a few rungs, you may find somebody who's easier and more pleasant for you to deal with.

Another thing to consider concerning the kind of prospect is this: if your prospects are powerful, important people they will help you in your career even if you change industries. Powerful people have a way of coming in handy no matter where your career takes you.

With many products, your prospect may be a teacher. Publishing jobs often require that you call on teachers or people with teaching backgrounds. If you like this sort of person—if, perhaps, you were once a teacher yourself—and if you don't look like a "sales-type," then you may find this environment particularly comfortable.

If you end up dealing with purchasing agents you'll discover that they don't care at all about a creative sales approach. They want to know what the product does and how much it costs. They'll take your bid, compare it with other bids, and try to determine which one—based on price and quality—will be their best buy. Once again, you have to determine whether or not this situation matches your talent and interests.

Aisle clerks are influential in all consumer products. An aisle clerk can sometimes be obtuse. He may not understand why the Johnson & Johnson Baby Shampoo should be stacked with the baby products *and* with the shampoos. And if you talk to him the same way you talk to the president of the company, he'll never help you. Where he puts your product on a shelf and how well he keeps it stocked can determine your sales volume. If you can get along with him, buy him a Coke every now and then, he'll end up being a great asset.

The fashion district in New York City is often thought of as a tough-talking, hard-pinching territory. If you're the kind of woman who can deal with the men you might encounter on

Seventh Avenue, then you might have a good time in the industry. If you know that that kind of environment is likely to make you feel tense and uncomfortable, then you should avoid a job that immerses you in it.

If your product requires that you call on liquor stores or bars and restaurants, then you have to consider how comfortable you are in a drinking milieu. You may have to deal with people who'll want you to sit at the bar with them at nine in the morning to sample the banana liqueur. Banana liqueur, first thing in the morning, doesn't go down like a Bloody Mary at Sunday brunch.

The financial district—Wall Street and its national outlets—is very receptive to women. Finance used to be perceived as a male domain, and it was anticipated that women would not be well received. Initially, there was a negative peer reaction from male *brokers,* but *prospects* have always been totally receptive.

As you examine the various industries with regard to the type of prospect, it's important for you to keep in mind that there isn't a "good kind" or a "bad kind." Imagine yourself in the selling situation. The only thing that matters is that you deal with people who don't make you feel uncomfortable. It's a totally subjective decision.

Prospect's Reception of Your Presentation

Ideally, every time you call for an appointment you'd get it, and every appointment you got would result in a sale. But that ideal has very little to do with reality. In reality there are two ratios that are important in sales. First is the ratio of how many people you need to call in order to get an appointment (Calls : Appointments). If you call ten people for every three appointments you get, you have a pretty reassuring ratio. If you have to call twenty people to get only one appointment you may get discouraged.

The second ratio is how many sales you make for each appointment (Sales : Appointments). If you had to make ten phone calls to get one appointment, and if you made three sales for every ten appointments you had, you've had to be involved with a hundred people in order to close three sales. If you had to make twenty appointments to get one sale, and it took you twenty calls to get each appointment, then you've had to speak with four hundred people to get just one sale.

It may be that each call only takes you three minutes. Or it may be that you're selling such sophisticated, expensive equipment that only four sales a year will insure you of earning $30,000. Whatever the specifics are, it's important for you to have an idea of these two ratios before you enter an industry. Of course, it can happen that the ratios are both staggeringly low for a year until you hit it right, and then everything can open up.

I have a friend who cracked the cosmetics and fragrance category for a major publication. He was a cosmetics salesperson and was hired to get a cosmetics and fragrance manufacturer to advertise in his paper. He went for three years without getting a single sale. He averaged, during those three years, three appointments a day, fifteen appointments a week, seven hundred and fifty appointments a year. He gave twenty-two hundred sales presentations, all with equal power, intelligence and enthusiasm, before he got his first sale. For the last seven years my friend has not earned less than $125,000 a year!

But it takes a special kind of confidence to keep going that way until you're successful. Think about yourself. How long would you be able to continue sounding confident if you didn't make a sale. You might be the same kind of person as my friend. He was absolutely certain that it was "just a matter of time" before he broke through. And he was right.

The nature of the selling situation is the most important consideration for any job. Consider it carefully.

Life-Style of the Selling Situation

There are some very high paying jobs—$40,000, $50,000, $60,000 a year—where you make six or seven appointments a day with no frills attached. You go out and give your presentation, they buy (or don't buy), you write the order, and you're finished. There are other jobs that have a lot of glamour. You may be expected to give only three sales presentations a day and one of them will be around a two-hour lunch. You may go to a spectacularly elegant restaurant, where the client lunch will run about $50, and then meet someone else in the early evening for drinks. You have to determine which life-style you identify with. How meaningful is the life-style to you?

If you're a Christian Scientist or an alcoholic who doesn't want to drink, then you won't want to make a sale over a martini. If you've been fighting a weight problem for ten years, the last thing you're going to need is the kind of job that requires you to have long lunches five days a week. If you have family obligations that require your presence in the home every day from four o'clock through the evening, you have to take that into account. And if you're just out of college, or recently divorced with grown children and no home responsibility, a heavy business/social schedule could be a terrific way to meet people and have fun.

Promotional Opportunity

Find out about the nature of promotions. By this I mean how frequently you're likely to be promoted, whether you get a change of title and a change of salary, and whether or not a promotion implies a change of location. You may work for a company that won't have many managerial openings in your home city. You can usually investigate that before you take a job.

Make it a point to go after *line promotions*—promotions into jobs that still involve your bringing money into your company. There are occasions when you might be tempted into a dead-end staff job, and you have to be astute enough to recognize those promotions for what they are. It's never too soon to think about your next move. Bobby Fischer, one of the world's great chess players, is alleged to be able to anticipate his plays twenty-three moves ahead. You might be better off if your employer gives you a top territory rather than a manager's seat. Never lose sight of your goals. A step to the side may turn out to be a step backward.

Degree of Pressure

No one wants heavy pressure. You can't sell with a lump in your throat the size of a grapefruit. You give good sales presentations when you're relaxed. There are ways to detect whether or not the job you're interested in is high-pressured.

Many sales forces are organized around the premise that the sales manager will have minimal control of his force. On such sales forces it's just impossible to keep track of how many calls a day each sales representative is making, and whether or not they're really doing everything that they could be doing. If you've ever been to an afternoon movie you may have noticed that several of the men in the theater are carrying little black suitcases. You can be sure that the theater isn't filled with doctors who don't want to be caught unprepared. Those men are salesmen, and at the end of the day they'll tell their sales managers that they were out all day calling on clients.

Since those sales managers have no way of judging how their sales representatives are spending the day, they may say things like, "If you don't make five sales a week, you're out!" Since there's no way to substantiate activity in those situations (e.g., selling door to door) the sales force is usually motivated by fear and reward. If you make ten sales a week you'll get a big carrot—MONEY. You want to avoid, at all costs, finding yourself on a sales force like the one I've just described.

A good way to avoid that sort of employment is to check the degree of annual turnover on a sales force before you join it. You can't ask, in an interview, if there's a lot of pressure on the job without sounding like someone who doesn't want to work hard. But you can draw your own conclusions when you're told what the turnover rate is. If there's a 25 percent turnover (with all of those people leaving the company, as opposed to going into management), then you know that something's wrong.

Location of Branches and Divisions

I touched on this criterion before when I discussed the category of Promotional Opportunity. Some women are circumstantially temperamentally suited to relocation. Others are not. You know what your social contracts are and you know what you can or cannot do. If you can relocate, then you should make a point of looking to those industries that pay a premium for that capability. If you find the idea of living in a new place exciting, *don't* go for jobs that will limit you to your current area.

If you're going to investigate companies that offer the possibility of relocation—and most big companies offer that possibility—check out the locations of the company's branches. If you live in a small town and are eager to move to a big city, then don't go to work for a company that has all of its offices in small towns. If you're eager to move into a small town, then reverse what I've just said. You must ask yourself, "If I join this company with the idea of eventually relocating, am I going to like the places they may end up sending me?" Think ahead. This isn't just another job—it's a career that you're planning.

Size of Industry

It is usually more desirable from your point of view to get involved with a big industry—not necessarily a big company, but a big industry. Big industries offer more to potential employees. If you go to work for one of the two companies in the country that manufacture a specific kind of product, you'll have only one other place to go with your acquired expertise if you leave your job. If you go into an industry like pharmaceuticals, however, you'll have the choice of 150 major pharmaceutical companies to work for over the course of your career. If you aren't offered a managerial position in one of those companies, you'll still have an opportunity with the other 149.

Visibility

If you are the first and only saleswoman on a sales force of eighty-five you will be referred to as "the woman." Everything you do will be duly noted and observed because it's being done by *the* woman. If you join a sales force where there are already eight women it will be easier to keep a low profile.

There's a pro and a con to visibility. Obviously, if you do well and you're highly visible, everyone will know about it. The other side of that coin is the negative aspect of high visibility. If you fail, everyone still knows about it. And lots of people are delighted to see a woman fail!

If you don't want that kind of notoriety, stay away from highly visible jobs. But in this case, just as with each of the other evaluative criteria, you have to take your personality into account. You may be the kind of person who shines when she's the center of attention. For many women that sort of focus is a great motivating force. For others it's paralyzing.

Average Raises over Twenty Years

Women have a tendency to be very shortsighted when it comes to career planning. Despite all of the changes in our culture, many women are still looking for jobs—not for careers. As I said earlier (and as I'll continue to stress throughout this book), looking for a career means thinking in terms of "Where will I be twenty years from now?"

There are jobs in which you will accumulate more business, make more money, and continue to advance just by staying on them. The starting deal may not be very enticing, but in terms of long-range career goals it may be a number one sales job. Insurance is one such field.

These areas of sales should not be ruled out because you want to make a "killing" fast. If you're the kind of persistent, patient person who has very serious ideas about a career-oriented life, it may be well worth the postponed gratification to get into one of these long-term growth fields.

Recession Sensitivity

Public relations and advertising—two areas that generally attract women—are very recession-sensitive. All support services of sales get cut out at the first sign of recession. In 1974 a major advertising agency in New York let go of 50 percent of its total staff! But no corporation ever fires the sales force. There's never been a board of directors meeting where the chairman stands up and says, "We have to put this corporation out of its misery. Let's fire the top salesmen." A good salesperson can *always* get a job in any kind of economy.

Financial Stability of the Company

If a company goes bankrupt, you won't get paid. It's important to devote your energies to a financially stable company. You don't have to check out or worry about any of the Fortune 500 companies. You can presume stability. But if you go for an interview with a little company that has no rugs on the floor, you have no assurance of how long they'll be around. Obviously, you can't ask the head of a company whether or not they're financially secure. You have to use your own skills of observation and draw your own conclusions. But it's a serious consideration in sales. If you don't get your commission until the end of the year, you want to be absolutely certain that your company is solvent when your "cash-in" time comes.

Entrepreneurial Possibilities

There are certain industries where you learn things that have direct, specific entrepreneurial applicability. If you learn how to sell advertising space you're learning one third of all you'll ever need to know to start your own publication. (You need to know circulation, editorial and advertising in order to start any magazine.)

If you work for the Ford Motor Company you may be learning managerial skills, or some other skills that have some kind of general application, but it's unlikely that in ten years you'll be able to go back to your hometown and start your own motor company.

The American Dream is to own your own business. In fact, there's good reason to want to be your own boss. Yet most people presume that the best thing in life is to work for someone else. "Who needs all the headaches when you can have a good income without them?" is how the reasoning usually goes.

Women are forever being discouraged by others at the idea of working for themselves. Consider the possibilities carefully. If you're interested in eventually owning your own business, then you must consider how the sales job you're applying for will affect the possibility of that ultimate goal. Even if you feel only the flicker of an attraction for being your own boss, you should make your career moves with that interest in mind.

What Suits You Now, and What Will Suit You in the Future

The idea of entrepreneurial potential brings us to a very important issue—the future you. Women going into sales for the first time must consider how their attitude is likely to change after a year or two of experience. Ideally, you should anticipate that you'll gain confidence with experience. Don't reject an offer now because it seems a bit intimidating—a bit over your head. You want to be able to grow into your job. If you take a job that doesn't make you even the least bit nervous—a job that you think will be a snap—then you're likely to be bored in a few months. Give yourself the benefit of the doubt. If you don't, no one else will.

Training

Everyone asks, "Does the company have training programs?" "What industries have training programs?" A woman who does not have sales experience will be trained by *any* corporation that's going to hire her. They hire you *expecting* you to know only what your background implies you will know. You will be trained about your product, and if you don't have sales experience, they'll give that to you as well. It *behooves* a company to have a good training program. That program may vary from industry to industry in terms of its length and its emphasis.

National Cash Register has a full year training program for its sales representatives. Other corporations will train you in three days and rely more heavily on on-the-job training.

Try to think about what kind of program you'd be most comfortable with before you begin to apply for jobs. In general, if you were a poor student, avoid long training programs.

Don't get hysterical the night before an interview because of what you *don't* know. Remember, good saleswomen are not trained—they simply are taught to apply a talent that's all their own!

6

Which Industry Is Best for You?

The following detailed charts are designed to give you a great deal of information about the major industries at a glance. This information has never before been published. All of the information is based on my own experience and business associations.

Look over the charts carefully and weigh all the factors before you make a decision. You should base your choice on a composite picture rather than on salary or any single aspect.

As you read the charts, keep referring to the section on "Selecting a Career Path in Sales." Much of the charts are written in shorthand with that section in mind.

Also, pay attention to the sections on life-style and attitude toward women. The most luxurious of the life-styles is in selling advertising space. But space sales will usually limit you to a big city. If you're living in the country with a husband and a couple of kids, you'll have very few potential employers.

Each industry offers something different, and each industry requires something different. As long as you're in a trainee position you can move from industry to industry. Once you begin to step up in the pecking order, your skills will become more specialized and your mobility more limited. After a while, if you change industries, you probably have to take a salary cut. So make certain before you move up too far that you like where you're headed!

INDUSTRY	STARTING INCOME	BENEFITS*
Auto	$85–125 per week + % ($13,000–17,000 first year)	minimum + car
Brokerage	$11,000–18,000 first year against or + %	big, less dental
Consumer	$10,000–13,000 + bonus (average bonus $600–1,200)	big + car
Cosmetics	$9,000–10,000 + bonus (average bonus $500)	average + car
Fashion (showroom)	$10,000–15,000	minimum + clothing discount
Industrial	$12,000–14,000 = % or bonus (average bonus $1,000)	average + car
Insurance	$8,000–18,000 against %	average, heavy insurance
Office Equipment	$12,000–15,000 against or + % (average bonus $2,000–5,000)	big
Commercial Real Estate	$125 per week against or + % ($10,000–15,000 first year)	minimal
Fashion (non-showroom)	$12,000–15,000 + bonus (average bonus $1,000)	average
Publishing	$10,500–13,000 + bonus (average bonus $500)	average + car
Space Sales	$10,000–15,000 + bonus (average bonus $2,000–5,000)	minimum to average
Pharmaceuticals	$11,000–13,000 + semi-annual review (review $1,500–3,000)	excellent + car

* Big = health, pension, profit sharing, dental, life insurance, long vacation, tuition reimbursement; average = health, pension, life insurance, long vacation; minimum = Blue Cross/Blue Shield.

INDUSTRY	TRAVEL	TRAVEL/EXPENSE ALLOWANCE	ATTITUDE TO WOMEN
Auto	none	none	poor
Brokerage	none	none	fair
Consumer	local	no meals	good
Cosmetics	regional 20%	fair	good
Fashion (showroom)	none	none	good
Industrial	heavy 20%–50%	fair to good	fair
Insurance	local	none	fair
Office Equipment	local	none	good
Commercial Real Estate	local	none	fair
Fashion (non-showroom)	regional national 25%	fair	poor
Publishing	regional (no overnight)	fair	fair
Space Sales	local regional 25%	excellent	good
Pharmaceuticals	local	none to minimal	good

INDUSTRY	LIFE-STYLE	PROMOTION OPPORTUNITY	PRESSURE	VISIBILITY
Auto	no entertaining no glamour	little to none	little to none	great
Brokerage	rare entertaining	little to none	little to average	good
Consumer	rare entertaining	excellent	little to none	fair
Cosmetics	rare entertaining	fair	little	none
Fashion (showroom)	rare entertaining	little to none	little to none	none
Industrial	rare entertaining	good	average	great
Insurance	rare entertaining	little	average to heavy	fair

INDUSTRY	LIFE-STYLE	PROMOTION OPPORTUNITY	PRESSURE	VISIBILITY
Office Equipment	rare entertaining	fair	average to heavy	fair
Commercial Real Estate	rare entertaining	little to none	little	good
Fashion (non-showroom)	good	fair	average	great
Publishing	rare entertaining	good	average	fair
Space Sales	excellent	fair	average	good
Pharmaceuticals	no entertaining	good	little	fair

INDUSTRY	BRANCH LOCATIONS	RELOCATION DEMAND	ENTREPRENEURIAL POTENTIAL
Auto	everywhere	none	good (own dealership)
Brokerage	everywhere	none	not applicable
Consumer	limited	little	not applicable
Cosmetics	limited	none	not applicable
Fashion (showroom)	none	none	not applicable
Industrial	little to average	average	not applicable
Insurance	everywhere	little	good (own agency)
Office Equipment	everywhere	average	not applicable
Commercial Real Estate	none	none	good
Fashion (non-showroom)	little	little	not applicable
Publishing	major cities	little	not applicable
Space Sales	minimal	none	unlikely (could start own magazine)
Pharmaceuticals	everywhere	minimal	not applicable

INCOME GROWTH

INDUSTRY	THIRD YEAR	FIFTH YEAR	TENTH YEAR
Auto	$22,000	$22,000–25,000	$22,000–35,000
Brokerage	$23,000–25,000	$35,000–40,000	$35,000–60,000
Consumer	$20,000	$20,000–25,000	$20,000–30,000
Cosmetics	$15,000–17,000	$15,000–20,000	$15,000–25,000
Fashion (showroom)	$10,000–18,000	$10,000–18,000	$10,000–18,000
Industrial	$20,000–25,000	$30,000–35,000	$30,000–50,000
Insurance	$20,000–25,000	$30,000–60,000	$30,000–100,000
Office Equipment	$20,000–30,000	$25,000–45,000	$30,000–50,000
Commercial Real Estate	$20,000–30,000	$25,000–40,000	$25,000–60,000
Fashion (non-showroom)	$25,000–30,000	$30,000–35,000	$30,000–60,000
Publishing	$20,000–25,000	$20,000–35,000	$25,000–45,000
Space Sales	$22,000–30,000	$30,000–50,000	$40,000–60,000
Pharmaceuticals	$17,000–23,000	$23,000–35,000	$33,000–45,000

NATURE OF SELLING SITUATION

INDUSTRY	HOW TO MEET PROSPECT	TYPE OF PROSPECT	RECEPTION TO PRODUCT/ SERVICE	SELLING ENVIRONMENT
Auto	75% walk-in; 25% appts.	consumer	comfortable	showroom
Brokerage	leads; phone; speeches; social	up-scale, mostly male	heavy lead develop. to start; service clients 1–2 yrs. = 75%	telephone
Consumer	service accts.	store mgr.; aisle clerk; acct. mgr.	comfortable	store

INDUSTRY	HOW TO MEET PROSPECT	TYPE OF PROSPECT	RECEPTION TO PRODUCT/ SERVICE	SELLING ENVIRONMENT
Cosmetics	cold calling	store buyer; store owner	fair	store
Fashion (showroom)	buyer comes to saleswoman	store buyer; store owner	comfortable	showroom
Industrial	cold calling; phone appts.	purchasing agt.	fair to good	client's office
Insurance	phone appts.	consumer	resistant	client's office; client's home
Office Equipment	cold calling	office mgr.; executive	resistant to fair	client's office; showroom
Commercial Real Estate	canvassing; referral	up-scale to mid-management	comfortable to fair	client's premises
Fashion (non-showroom)	appts.; cold calling	store buyer	comfortable	client's premises
Publishing	cold calling	teacher; bookstore mgr.	fair to resistant	schools; bookstores
Space Sales	appts.; servicing accounts	ad agencies; media buyer; marketing director	comfortable to fair	offices; restaurants
Pharmaceuticals	cold calling	doctors; hospitals	comfortable	doctor's office

INDUSTRY	SIZE & QUALITY OF SALES FORCE*	TRAINING
Auto	small poor	on the job
Brokerage	large average to good	excellent
Consumer	large average to good	excellent
Cosmetics	large average	fair

INDUSTRY	SIZE & QUALITY OF SALES FORCE*	TRAINING
Fashion (showroom)	small average	little, informal
Industrial	small good	excellent
Insurance	large average	fair to poor
Office Equipment	large good	excellent
Commercial Real Estate	small fair to poor	fair to poor
Fashion (non-showroom)	small good	good
Publishing	average fair	excellent
Space Sales	small to average good	on the job
Pharmaceuticals	large average	excellent

* Small = up to 8; Average = 9–20; Large = 20+

CHAPTER

7

Venturing Out

Whenever we send someone out on an interview from Careers For Women we call up the interviewer when it's over and ask for his impressions. We've learned from this feedback that many of you will lose the opportunity to get a job for which you're well qualified—a job that you very much want—because you don't know how to take a sales interview.

As a result of this feedback we also know *why* people *don't* get hired, and our information can help you avoid the pitfalls of the job search. Sales is, as I've said before, a male-dominated area of business, and before you can get hired for a good sales job you may have to educate the person who's doing the hiring. Not too long ago I received the following letter from the head of a corporation. Its contents should give you some idea of what you may be up against.

> *Dear Mr. King:*
> *We were pleased to learn that you might be another source of sales talent for our corporation. Let me give*

you some idea of who we consider to be the ideal sales manager.

We are looking for men between the ages of 22 and 40 who are emotionally mature, responsible, practical, and able to face facts and deal with difficult situations independently.

Ideally we like our men to be married with children and to have a well-rounded home life. Their interests and outside activities should show evidence of their ability to get along with people.

Finally, we are looking for men whose job history indicates stability and upward mobility. We know that it's unlikely that we'll find one man with all of the above specifications, but we want you to be aware of our evaluative criteria.

There is a lot to be learned from the above letter. Aside from the obvious fact that he used the word "men" four times, there are other, more subtle ways in which the letter discriminates against women. Consider, for example, that this interviewer is looking for men with children. Every employer would prefer, if they *have* to hire women, to hire women without children. Somehow the very things that indicate a man's stability and emotional maturity work in reverse for women.

Women also encounter problems because employers are looking for people with stable job histories. Unlike men, most women don't go to college with the intention of getting vocational preparation. Bright women who major in Art History, Eighteenth-Century English Literature, or Spanish usually discover—when they're faced with the proposition of supporting themselves—that the only jobs for which they're qualified involve typing, filing or answering the phone.

Those same bright women who take those jobs also find that after six months their brains are turning to mush and they're desperate to *get out*. Since most of those jobs aren't preparation for anything but more dull jobs the entire process often repeats itself, and many intelligent women end up with very spotty résumés. The irony of these résumés is that they indicate positive rather than negative things, and men in hiring positions have to be trained to read them properly. You, on the other hand, have to be trained to write them properly, and that's what we're about to do.

The Résumé

Most job seekers don't really understand the importance of a résumé. The résumé is only one-twentieth as important as the interview. Since most job seekers overestimate the power of a résumé, I suspect that the reason for this overemphasis is that you can always get someone else to do your résumé for you. If you keep getting turned down for jobs, and you keep getting new people to redo your résumé, you can, quite effectively, avoid taking a good hard look at yourself.

In reality your interview is much more of a decisive factor as to whether or not you get hired than your résumé is. The résumé is important, but it's important in a different way than an interview. A good résumé serves two purposes: first, it gets you an interview, and second, it might be used as a guideline for your interview.

Make Your Résumé Look Different

Assume that you've just come across the following advertisement in your newspaper:

Wanted: Saleswoman with no experience. Prior background unimportant. Must be willing to travel internationally, mostly to Europe three months a year. All ex-

penses paid plus guaranteed base salary of $18,000. Box 200Z.

To most of us that sounds like a pretty good job. That job description is, in fact, so appealing that your résumé will probably be one of several hundred to appear in Box 200Z the following day!

Whoever opens Box 200Z has no intention of interviewing several hundred job applicants. More likely, he'll go through the résumés and pick a dozen people to interview. If no one in that first dozen works out, he'll return to his pile of résumés and select another twelve applicants. Obviously it's to your mathematical advantage to be one of the first twelve people interviewed and it's up to you when you prepare a résumé to prepare it in such a way that it stands out from all the rest.

How do you do that? One thing you might consider is having your résumé printed (or typed) on a slightly tinted stock. If one hundred and ninety-nine résumés are on white paper and one résumé is on beige paper, the beige one is going to stand out. Someone might say, "Let's interview the one who sent in the beige résumé." You're supplying an interviewer with a frame of reference. Don't, however, print your résumé on a lurid or deep-colored paper, and don't do anything that screams out femininity . . . like pink stock with a flowered border. There's a fine line between being different and being unprofessional, and you have to tread that line carefully.

If you're having someone print up a hundred copies of your résumé you can assume that they're going to use their cheapest stock (paper). It's to your advantage to ask them to use a heavier paper for your résumé, even if you have to go out and buy the paper for them. Heavy paper feels different from what most printers use on résumés, and a future employer will notice the difference as he thumbs through the ream.

Finally, you should consider the possibility of attaching a picture to your résumé. Although pictures have, in the past, been used as a means of discriminating against minority groups, there are some ways in which it can work to your advantage. If you have a pleasant appearance (not necessarily pretty but alert and intelligent-looking) and your résumé is one of several hundred, your picture will give an interviewer the feeling that he knows something extra about you. He'll feel a bit more familiar with you than he does with all of the faceless applicants.

There are a number of ways that you can include your photograph with your résumé. The most impressive is to have a picture of yourself silk-screened into the upper right-hand corner. Whoever prints your résumé can advise you about silk-screening.

What to Include

The most important thing to remember when you prepare your résumé is that nothing should be included on it unless it will improve your chances of getting an interview. Don't fill up your sheet of paper with all sorts of extraneous material. Every word on your résumé should have a purpose, and that purpose is to get you in the door.

There are a variety of résumé formats, but the only one I recommend is called a chronological résumé. This most widely accepted format is also the easiest to write. Both your work experience and your education are listed in chronological order, starting with the most recent—which also gets the most detailed attention—and working back through the years.

Read the following chronological résumé very carefully.

Susan Sands
123 West 4th Street
New York, N.Y.
555-3427

Height: 5'5"
Weight: 112 lbs.
Health: Excellent
Marital Status: Single
Age: 30

EDUCATION

COLUMBIA GRADUATE
SCHOOL OF BUSINESS
—M.B.A., May 1976
—Marketing and Finance
  Concentration
—Member, American Marketing
  Association
—Member, American Finance
  Association

DUKE UNIVERSITY
GRADUATE SCHOOL OF
ARTS AND SCIENCES
—M.A., December, 1970
—Ford Foundation Fellowship

UNIVERSITY OF VIENNA,
AUSTRIA
—East-West Cultural Exchange
  Program, Summer, 1971
—Scholarship

DUKE UNIVERSITY
—B.A., June, 1965
—Ford Foundation Honors-
  Master's Program
—Dean's List all semesters

EMPLOYMENT

2/77–present   KWIK-PRINT INC., New York, N.Y.
Printing Sales Rep
—Sell to major corporations, advertising agencies and designers. Only saleswoman on national staff of 26. Developed 23 major accounts in first seven months and exceeded annual quota by 200% without leads or existing clients. Established such prestigious new clients as Revlon, Family Circle, S & H, and Taylor Industries. Projected business-life expectancy of these accounts to be in excess of $1,000,000.

11/74–2/77   ANCHOR INDUSTRIES, New York, N.Y.
Public Relations Assistant
—Planned and placed financial news releases for distribution to specific target audiences. Had direct responsibility for researching and writing press announcements and functional brochures for all general public relations areas. Organized and participated as corporate representative for a variety of conventions and meetings.

2/72–9/74	GARON CHEMICALS, New York, N.Y.
	Customer Relations Director
	—Primary responsibility was to insure smooth transition for new franchises. Acted as liaison between home office and district directors.

INTERESTS	*Debating, Competitive Skiing, Travel, Chess*

References will be furnished upon request.

Personal Data

The first part of your résumé should include any personal data that will work in your favor. You will always have to include your name, address and home telephone number.

If you look at Susan Sands's résumé, you'll see that she's included a good deal of information in addition to her address and phone number. Susan Sands is a composite of a number of people I've dealt with, and for the purpose of illustration I've given her the strongest possible résumé. If all of your personal data spells out as well as Susan's does you should include it.

For the sake of clarity I want to specify what "good" personal data means. Your height and weight should indicate that you present a good appearance. You needn't be Sophia Loren. (You should never give statistics other than height and weight.) But your statistics should make it clear that you're neither obese nor scrawny. They should give an interviewer some indication of your appearance so that he feels a bit more familiar with you than he would otherwise.

If your health is good, include it. If you have any problem with your health you should omit the category entirely. Never say anything negative about yourself.

Don't ever put down your marital status if you are married, or if you're separated. In either of those two instances the place to discuss your status is the interview. If you write down "married" an interviewer will be concerned about the issue of children and your husband's attitude toward your working, traveling, etc. If you write down "separated" most people will assume that you're in the midst of a great deal of emotional stress and a bad hiring risk. "Single" is not going to be ideal for all jobs, but it incurs the least prejudice. If you're divorced leave it off.

If you think back to the letter I quoted earlier from the head of a corporation you'll recall that he specified his preference that sales*men* "be married with children." The fact that the preferences regarding marital status are precisely the opposite for men as they are for women should give you some idea of how deeply entrenched are most employers' attitudes toward sex roles in our culture. You can't ignore this bias, but if you're smart you can get around it.

Never, under any circumstances, include anything on your résumé about children. Once you get your interview the question of children will undoubtedly arise—preferably you'll be the one to bring it up—but until then it shouldn't even be an issue.

Generally, anyone who falls outside the age range of twenty-five to forty will be at a disadvantage. If your age falls anywhere within these brackets it's to your advantage to include it on your résumé. An age that's somewhere between twenty-five and forty tells an employer that you have a good twenty years ahead of you in your work life, and that it's to his advantage to invest in training you. If you leave your age off a résumé there will be an implication that you're hiding something.

If, as you read this, you're thinking, "Hey. I don't have to include any of this stuff. They have no legal right to know my age or anything else about my personal life," you're absolutely right. Legally speaking no one can turn you down for a job because you're older, overweight, underweight, or separated. But you have to be very clear on what your purpose is.

If your purpose in applying for jobs is to get a job, you have to be smart. Any information that will work in your favor should be on your résumé; and that includes height, weight, health, marital status and age . . . *if* it works in your favor.

You'll have to determine whether to follow your personal data with "education" or with "employment." If you have a very strong educational background, as Susan Sands does, then you'd be wise to lead with it. If your educational background is weak but your work experience can translate into good selling talent, then that's where you should begin. If you start with your strengths, then your weaknesses will be read in light of your strong points. If you start with your weaknesses, there is a chance that the interviewer may discard your résumé and you from consideration without ever getting to your strong points.

Education

The best format for listing your educational achievements is to begin with the highest level and designate the school, degree and year in that order just as it is on Susan Sands's résumé. If you never got a degree but have some college credit, note the school and the years of your attendance (City University, 1965–1967). Never write anything like "Partial college," or "Did not fulfill degree requirements." Remember, the rule of résumé writing is NEVER SAY ANYTHING ABOUT YOURSELF THAT ISN'T POSITIVE.

If you haven't completed college don't list your high school in an effort to fill out the page. The only time you should designate your high school is if it's a special prestigious school or if you were the recipient of some very special honors or awards.

If you have several degrees you'll have to decide whether or not to list your area of specialization. My experience indicates that unless your area of specialization is in some way tied into sales or business, you're better off not listing it. If you have an advanced degree, put it down, and if you're working toward a graduate degree in something that has nothing to do with business, leave it off. You want your potential interviewer to think that business, and sales in particular, is your strongest current interest.

If you have no college credit or degree, you'll want your educational data to follow your employment data (which, hopefully, will be stronger). Never lie about a degree. College degrees are the easiest thing for a future employer to check out, and you're better off without a degree than you would be if you were caught in a fabrication.

Employment

With regard to format, your vocational background should be listed in very much the same way as your educational background. Look again at Susan Sands's résumé. The dates of her employment are listed in the left margin by month and year. On the right she's listed the name of each company that's employed her and the city in which she's worked. You needn't supply exact street addresses. Anyone who wants to check for the exact address or phone number can look it up in the phone book. Under the name of each company Susan has supplied her title. And directly under each title she's supplied the most important information of any résumé.

Describing Your Job

The most common error of résumé preparation involves *how* people describe their jobs. In order to do your job description justice you need to keep reminding yourself about your goals. Ultimately you're looking for a sales job. Any previous job that you've held must be described in a way that will enhance your chances of getting that sales job.

I'm convinced that women have a unique problem with the concept of "bragging." I'll go into more detail about this problem when I begin to discuss the interview, but it's germane to discuss it here in terms of how you're planning to describe your past employment. You must keep in mind that no one knows what you did in your past jobs. No one is going to read your descriptions and say, "My. What a perfect description she's given us of her last job. Let's hire her." You are not, in a word, going to be hired on the basis of how accurately you described your work history.

Much more important than job description is the concept of job accomplishments. When I first got Susan Sands's résumé her description of the Kwik-Print job read as follows:

Sold printing service to major corporations in the N.Y.C. area. Duties consisted of meeting clients, determining their needs and monitoring their job orders from conception to completion. Very frequently required to fly to Cincinnati to supervise actual printing.

Compare the above job description with the one that appeared on her final résumé. Every sentence in the earlier description succeeds in describing her job, yet not one sentence describes her personal accomplishments on the job. You have to learn to brag nicely if you expect to put together an effective résumé.

When I read the first version of Susan's résumé I asked her to describe what *she* had done to emphasize her accomplishments. When she told me she sold $165,000 in her first seven months I asked what the company had to do to blow an account once she had brought it in. She explained that most accounts stayed with Kwik-Print for about five years, unless the company really did a disastrous job on their printing.

If I multiplied the amount of work she'd brought in during her first seven months ($165,000) by five (the minimum number of years she could assume that her accounts would remain in the company) the projected life expectancy earnings came to $825,000. Since that figure only represents her first seven months it's reasonable to assume that by the end of a year it would be up to $1,000,000. That's an impressive figure, isn't it!

I once helped a woman named Elana put together her résumé. Four years earlier she had been an executive secretary earning $20,000 a year. She had co-signature power on twenty-five bank accounts. All of that was impressive and looked good on her résumé. She wrote: "Authority of co-signature on twenty-five bank accounts. Authority to directly initial any activity over the signature of the marketing manager." And she had about six or seven other very impressive sentences. Then she devoted three sentences to a part of her job that involved organizing lunch (i.e., making sandwiches, coffee, etc.) in the boardroom. The last three sentences of her job description left one with the impression that she was part secretary, part waitress, and totally demeaned her other responsibilities. They should have been left out.

There are psychological aspects to a résumé. If you spend half of your time doing customer liaison and other quasi-sales work and the other half of your time doing strictly clerical work, you should devote nine sentences to the first part and maybe one last sentence to the clerical work. Anyone who reads your résumé will think that nine tenths of your job is sales-related.

Interests

The rule about selectivity applies particularly to the section of your résumé on personal interests. Any hobby or interest that goes on your résumé should, in some way, reflect on your potential as a saleswoman. Susan Sands may spend every evening of her life sitting in her bedroom working on needlepoint, but you don't see "needlepoint" on her résumé. It's too isolating a hobby to translate well into sales.

Think about the things you like to do. If you have any interest or hobby that's an unusual area for women—hunting, woodworking, debating—include it on your résumé. It will indicate that you've already ventured into what people think of as a "man's world" and that you've had some success. Hopefully they'll think, "If she has the guts to make it on a safari how can she fail in sales?"

Of course the interests you list on your résumé needn't all be "masculine." If you like to act and occasionally work in amateur theater, put it down. If you're interested in any competitive sport, like tennis, or gymnastics, put it down. Even sports that aren't competitive, like skiing, will enhance a sales résumé. If you keep in mind that you want to project a people-oriented image you won't have any trouble slanting your résumé in that direction.

References

The rule about references on a résumé is very simple and easy to remember. Never list references. At the bottom of your résumé write, "References will be furnished upon request." If an employer is interested in you they'll ask for your references. Ideally, you'll have plenty of time to call up the people you want to use and get a sense of what they're going to say about you.

The worst thing that can happen is for a reference, or a former employer, to be taken by surprise. It's entirely possible that one of the companies listed on your résumé may have a new personnel director who never heard of you. In fact, the personnel director who hired you ten years earlier may have forgotten who you are. In either of those two instances a potential employer will call and ask about you and hear, "Susan Sands, Susan Sands. Let me see now," followed by a long pause. That sort of response doesn't make Susan Sands sound like the most dynamic person ever employed by the ABC Company.

You needn't feel uncomfortable about calling the personnel department of any company that's employed you and saying, "This is Susan Sands. I worked in the editorial department in 1969 and I've just included you on a current résumé. I just wanted to refresh your memory of me so that if anyone called, you wouldn't have a problem."

Finally, don't ever use someone as a reference unless you're 100 percent certain that they'll *only* say glowing things about you. It's shocking how many women feel that they need some "balance" in their references. There's something superstitious about thinking that if all of your references say terrific things about you a potential employer won't believe them, yet that sort of superstition enjoys a wide audience. The point of a reference is to make you look good. If you give a reference who does anything short of that your employer will think you're not a very desirable employee.

The Editing

Once you've got all the information down on paper, find yourself a comfortable chair and sit down to read your résumé. It's not a bad idea, at this point, to try and put yourself in the position of an employer. Read it as though you might consider hiring yourself.

Part of this sort of reading should result in some final polishing. Your résumé should look good. People who read résumés for a living take great exception at seeing an error in grammar and typing. They might be fussy about an uneven margin. Sales often involves a good deal of letter writing and if your résumé is poorly written they'll assume that you can't write a good letter.

After you've checked your résumé for any spelling or typographical errors read it once again to make certain that your parallel structure is right. The most common grammatical error on résumés usually involves what we call errors in parallelism. If three sentences on your résumé begin with a subject ("I was responsible for . . ."), then you must be certain that every sentence on your résumé includes a subject. If you elect to omit the subject ("Responsible for . . . Oversaw meetings . . ."), then make sure that the word "I" doesn't appear anywhere on your résumé. Either kind of sentence structure is fine as long as you're consistent.

But What About . . . ?

The two great "What abouts . . ." are salary and volunteer work. The question of salary has the easiest answer. Never, under any circumstances, include past salaries on your résumé. I'll discuss the issue of past salary when we get to the interview. It's entirely likely that the question of your past salaries will come up during an interview and unless you anticipate it and are prepared to deal with it you may lose several hundreds of thousands of dollars. And that's no exaggeration.

Volunteer work should only be included on a résumé if it enhances your sales appeal. Many women who are just joining the work force either have never had a job or haven't worked in twenty years. If, during the time you were raising a family you were involved in volunteer work that can translate into sales talent—fund-raising, community organizing, etc.— then you should list that work in the section of your résumé ordinarily reserved for employment. Since you never indicate salary on a résumé you needn't indicate (at that point) that you worked for nothing. Keep in mind that if your organization didn't have you there working for free they'd probably have to pay someone a good salary to do what you do.

If you've had a full-time job while you also did volunteer work, and if your volunteer work will enhance your image, then include it in the section of your résumé reserved for "interests." But remember, the only reason to include something on your résumé is because you think it will help you get an interview.

Sending It Out

Once you've completed your résumé you're ready to begin looking for a job. There are a number of ways you can look for a job in sales. Women who've been through our program usually get their jobs through us. If you live in a city that doesn't have a Careers For Women program you may want to work through an employment agency.

Or, you may just work with a newspaper. Every newspaper has, in its classified section, a list of available jobs in sales. Read through the section carefully and send your résumé to any job that sounds interesting. (Remember, don't apply for jobs that advertise "straight commission" unless you have absolutely no choice.) Don't get two hundred copies of your résumé printed and send them to every major industry in your area. Applying for jobs that don't exist will only wear down your ego.

Whenever you send out your résumé you should include a cover letter. The cover letter provides another opportunity for you to impress a future employer. It's almost like a personal introduction, and if it's well written it can give you the edge when it comes to deciding who gets an interview.

There are several things you should keep in mind when you write your cover letter. First, remember that this letter will be considered as a sample of your letter-writing skills. It should be typed in the standard business-letter format, and it should be read carefully for any errors in grammar, usage, or typing.

Every cover letter should be slanted for a particular job. It's always a good idea to do some research on the company before you send out your résumé, and to indicate some knowledge of the company in your cover letter. It's also important to consider the specific skills required in the job for which you're applying and to indicate any talent related to those skills in your letter.

Always limit your cover letter to a few paragraphs and never allow it to run over one page. The point of this letter is to underline the reason you're sending your résumé, to explain specifically why you think you'd excel at *that* job, and to get an interview. Your closing sentence should always be a request for that sought-after interview.

Consider the following letter that accompanied Susan Sands's résumé:

123 West 4th Street
New York, N.Y. 10005
September 12, 1978

Mr. James Clarence
Skiing Magazine
32 Park Ave., S.
New York, N.Y. 10016

Dear Mr. Clarence:

My experience in sales and business should be of interest to you in your search for a new space salesperson.

My résumé will indicate my experience in sales, as well as my specific experience in dealing with advertising agencies, designers and printers. As a subscriber to Skiing Magazine *and an avid skier I feel particularly interested in a position on your staff.*

I'm currently employed but will be on vacation all of next week and available to come and meet with you. I look forward to hearing from you.

Sincerely,

Susan Sands

Enc: Résumé

The Selling Interview

Your interview is the single most important factor in determining whether or not you get a job. There's a great deal to know about interviewing, and there's a great deal that you, as the interviewee, can control. The more you anticipate, the better you'll do.

It's important for you to understand that an interview always involves at least two people: you and the interviewer. And each of you has a purpose. The interviewer's purpose is to determine whether or not you, above the other candidates, should be offered the job. That's his exclusive purpose in interviewing you. He isn't there to make friends. He isn't there to determine whether or not you went to the same high school. No matter how friendly or chatty an interviewer is, you should never lose sight of what his purpose is.

Your purpose is, of course, to get a job *offer*. No matter what you hear during your job interview, you shouldn't let it affect your determination to get a job offer. I'll discuss specific games interviewers play later, but for now you should remember that once you get a job offer you'll have plenty of time to decide whether to accept it or turn it down.

Talking to a Stranger

The most difficult thing to keep in mind on a job interview is that you're talking to a stranger. Most of our time is spent talking with friends, relatives, friends of relatives, relatives of friends, or people with whom we have some sort of relationship. It's very rare that we're in a situation that requires lengthy discussion with a total stranger.

Think of what your impulse is when you find yourself sitting next to a stranger with time to kill. One of the games people most frequently play in that situation involves establishing connections. "Where did you grow up?" "Where is your family from?" "What school did you go to?" And finally, "Do you know . . . ?"

Most of us feel more comfortable talking with someone *after* we've established some common ground. But a job interview has such specific purposes and such limited time that most "getting to know you" games have to be overlooked. We are left, as I said, talking with a stranger, and when you talk with a stranger you're at a disadvantage. Let me give you an example of one problem.

If I come into my office on Monday morning and snarl at my secretary she'll probably assume that I had a rough weekend and am feeling kind of off. She'll know that I'm just not myself. If I have a Monday morning interview, having had the same rough weekend, and snarl at a group of strangers for an hour, they're going to think that I'm a snarler . . . or a weirdo . . . or someone they don't *need* on Monday morning.

The people in our social communities *know* us. They understand what we say even if we don't say it. The fact of the matter is that we all talk in a code. We leave things out.

We assume that people can fill in the background for us. Sigmund Freud said that we only know the tip of the iceberg when it comes to understanding personality. I prefer to think of myself as a loaf of bread. When I'm with friends I might show them one slice of bread but they'll have the rest of the loaf in mind. When I'm with a stranger I have to make sure that he either gets to know the whole loaf in a hurry or only sees my best slices!

In dealing with strangers it's helpful to keep reminding yourself that you are, in fact, strangers. Before you go into an interview, tell yourself that your interviewer knows nothing more about you than you've told him on your résumé. Once the interview begins, keep an eye on the person you're talking to. You have to make certain that he's hearing everything the way you want it to be heard.

If you're the kind of person who relies heavily on humor you want to be certain that your interviewer gets your jokes. If, as you get going, you notice that *he* isn't laughing, then you'd better be careful. You may be saying things lightly that he's taking quite seriously. You have to constantly evaluate how you're doing when you're talking with a stranger. Nothing can be taken for granted.

Everything that you say makes an impact on an interviewer, whether it is or isn't job-related. We once sent a woman named Margaret off to an interview with a client whom we knew very well. The client wanted to send the number one candidate to Michigan to be interviewed by the two midwestern managers. When they described the job to us they said that they needed someone who would be willing to relocate to suburban Detroit and that they wanted to make certain that whoever they hired would enjoy living out there.

This very same client had recently relocated someone to San Francisco. Nine months after they moved her she decided that she didn't like the West Coast. She caused them a great deal of embarrassment and cost them a lot of money.

Eventually they moved her back to New York, but they didn't want to make the same mistake twice.

Before we sent Margaret off to be interviewed I met with her personally to convince myself that she'd be happy living in Detroit. She explained that she'd spent a great deal of time in the area, that she used to have a boyfriend there, and that, strange as it may seem, she really was excited about going back there to live.

Everything she said sounded good, but I was still concerned that she might make a careless slip-up. I told her to be certain that if they asked about sports she didn't tell them the sort of stuff one did in Florida. Rather, I suggested, she should talk about backpacking around Lake Michigan, or water-skiing, or whatever it is that people in Detroit do. I warned her that the client was touchy about relocating and that she had to be on guard.

And off she went to Detroit to interview with George and Bill. She interviewed with George in the morning and called me after the interview to tell me how fantastically it had all gone. "In fact," she said, "I'm off now to have lunch with George, I'm going to meet Bill after we eat, and I expect to be on the four o'clock plane home." When I warned her to be careful about what she said during lunch, she said, "Please, David, relax. I'm telling you that I'm doing great."

Needless to say, that afternoon I got a call from my client saying that they had decided not to hire Margaret. They simply didn't feel convinced that she'd be happy living in suburban Detroit. When I asked him to explain further, he said that during lunch George had asked her how she liked living in New York.

Margaret's answer was passionate. She said, "You don't live in New York City. I'll tell you what you do in New York City. You get up in the morning and you cram yourself into a smelly subway train with a lot of people you wouldn't have lunch with or even talk to and you ride down to work and you go into a hateful disgusting thing in an area of town called Wall Street and by the time you leave it's dark and you're busy thinking about getting home without having someone hit you on the head and steal your wallet, and home is some laughable excuse for a room up three flights of stairs for $250," and she went on and on and on.

My client and Bill and George had all concluded that Margaret was much more eager to get out of New York than she was to come to Detroit. In fact, they felt that she hadn't really given much thought to things specific to Detroit. There is, after all, lots of crime in Detroit. Surely she didn't think those problems were peculiar to New York. And they also felt that anyone who had such a difficult time adjusting to life in one place probably wouldn't have an easy time adjusting to life somewhere else.

Where did Margaret go wrong? Primarily, she forgot she was lunching with a stranger; with someone who didn't know that she always had a tendency to exaggerate and to engage in theatrics. Apparently she forgot what the purpose of her luncheon was. If she had reminded herself that she was lunching with a stranger and that the purpose of the lunch was to get a job she might have responded differently. She might have said, "New York has a great deal to offer, particularly in terms of the arts, but, quite honestly, I'm not the kind of person to take public transportation. I grew up in the suburbs, and I like being able to get in my car to take care of things. That sort of option is much more feasible in any suburb than it is in New York."

Before You Get There

Before you go on an interview you'll want to give some consideration to what you're going to wear. When most men know they're going to be doing a lot of interviewing they buy what they call an *interview* suit. Women should have the equivalent of an *interview suit*. The best way to determine the appropriate dress for any given industry is to wait outside a company's offices at five o'clock one day and watch the women coming out. If most of the women are dressed conservatively, then you should dress in a like style for your interview.

Usually style of dress is consistent within an industry. If you want to interview for a job selling insurance in a big city you can assume that people in most insurance companies dress the same way. I'm not a fancy dresser. I tend to wear a variety of very casual outfits in my office. But when I go out to meet with a client I don't wear blue jeans and sandals. I have a very straight business suit that makes me look like the president of a company. My outfit cost me $450 and I consider that money well spent. When I go to meet a client in that suit I look successful, and we all tend to trust our business to successful-looking people.

You also have to be certain that your *interview suit* is pressed and clean on the morning of your appointment. The best way to be sure that you look good on an interview is to check your outfit three days in advance. That should allow you time to take care of falling hems, spots, runs in hosiery, and anything else.

Arriving

Another way to be certain that you look good for an interview is to arrive at least fifteen minutes early. If you're as much as five minutes late for an interview you should assume that you've lost the job. Most likely you know, better than anyone else, if your tendency is to be late. Always take that tendency into account when you calculate your trip to an interview. First, plan on arriving fifteen minutes before you're expected, and second, plan on hitting a lot of traffic en route. That combination should give you plenty of time.

When you arrive, find the precise door that will lead to your interview. Some personnel departments take up two floors of an office building and it can take ten minutes for you to find the person with whom you have an appointment. Once you've found the place, introduce yourself to the receptionist, tell her that you're early and would rather not be announced yet, and ask her for the key to the ladies' room.

The ladies' room is the place to relax (comb your hair, fix your collar, and make certain you have no lipstick on your teeth). The most important thing about arriving early is that it gives you this extra time to collect yourself. If you've had some time to yourself you can walk into your interview feeling confident. If you arrive "just in time" you'll be out of breath and disheveled when you meet your interviewer. First impressions count!

About Those Itches

You've just been ushered into the office of a man who will interview you. He stands as you enter and gestures toward a chair that faces his desk. He extends a hand, which you shake *firmly,* and introduces himself. You sit down. And that's when it usually happens. Your arm itches. Your leg itches. You move a hand up to your head and begin to scratch. Johnny Carson tends to rub his eye. Carol Burnett tugs her earlobe. A friend of mine taps his foot.

There are certain things you should not do on an interview. Every time you move a hand to your face your interviewer is going to watch that hand move, and if he's busy watching your hands he's going to have a hard time concentrating on what you're saying. Most experienced interviewers know that this is a nervous gesture. They've watched hundreds of people parade into their offices, touch their faces and scratch.

Unless you're careful you're likely to become just another

scratcher. If, on the other hand, you can sit through an interview with your hands poised in your lap, you'll succeed in conveying a different message: I'M NOT NERVOUS. An interviewer will notice if you are calm and poised.

Unfortunately you may have a hundred nervous gestures that you don't even know about. You might set a rule for yourself that you'll never touch yourself above the neck during an interview but continue to grit your teeth. You can avoid that sort of problem by asking someone you trust if you have any distracting gestures. A good friend will cue you in to your movement and you'll have an easier time staying aware of it. Keep a vigil on your body while you're interviewing.

Eye Contact

You also need to work to establish good eye contact. When an interviewer is talking you must have your eyes on him 100 percent of the time. When you're talking you must have your eyes on him 90 percent of the time. There's nothing wrong with looking away every now and then to collect your thoughts. Your tendency will be to do this right after you're asked a question. You'll look away, think for a moment, then return your eyes to the interviewer and begin talking. Good eye contact doesn't mean eyeball to eyeball. You can establish good eye contact during an interview by looking, in a general way, at someone's face. You can look at your interviewer's nose, mouth or cheeks and still establish the impression of good eye contact.

If you know that you're the kind of person who can't help but let your eyes wander you needn't despair. Anyone can learn to establish good eye contact. Work at it. Make a discipline of it. Practice it with all your friends, with the waitresses in your favorite restaurant. Make yourself conscious of it and after about two weeks it will come naturally. Re-

member, good eye contact is important in sales even beyond
your initial interview. It's an integral part of any sales presentation.

Unfair Questioning

I mentioned earlier that many interviewers use your
résumé as a guide for their interview. The first part of your
résumé involves your personal data, and you may recall that I
alluded to interview problems with regard to that information.
I know of a woman who wrote on her résumé that she was
divorced. An interviewer once looked at the sheet of paper
before him and said, "I see here that you're divorced. Tell me.
Who dumped whom?"

It's hard to remain poised when a total stranger vul-
garizes the most traumatic episode of your life. In this case, it
was none of his business what the circumstances surrounding
her divorce were. Whether or not she found lipstick on her
husband's collar doesn't have anything to do with her potential in sales. The interviewer might have asked the question to
see how well she did under stress, or he may have been just
plain nosy. Whatever his motivations, the question was inappropriate. Nonetheless, remember that *you* have to be prepared to cope with inappropriate questions.

What do you do? Let's examine some alternatives. If you
were to say, "I really don't see where that's any of your business," you would be saying, in essence, "I don't want this job."
Since I believe that the goal of a job interview is to get a job
offer (remember, you can always turn a job down once it's
been offered), I don't put much stock in that response.

Probably the best response to that sort of question is, "It
was a mutual decision and an amicable divorce. He's a great
guy but we just weren't great together." That sort of answer
tells the interviewer what he wants to hear: that you don't hate

men; that you don't have reason to hate men; and that you can deal with disappointment.

But what if that's not true? What if your husband was a bum who came home drunk and who generally treated you terribly? Well, those questions bring us to the issue of discretion during an interview. And discretion is a loaded issue for women. Somehow women, more than men, feel that if they don't "tell all" they're lying. That feeling frequently leads women to help future employers take advantage of them.

Given the fact that an interviewer has no right to ask inappropriate questions, why should a woman be obligated to answer them? The onus is on the unfair questioner. *He* doesn't *deserve* a candid answer. And *you* don't *deserve* to hurt your chance at a job.

Money

Money is the subject of a great deal of unfair questioning. An interviewer will ask, in the most matter-of-fact voice, what your last salary was. And women will invariably feel that they have to answer. The matter of your past salaries is privileged information. If you want to check on just how privileged this information is, I suggest that you try an experiment.

Call the personnel department where you last worked and say that you're calling from another personnel department and that you're interested in hiring yourself. Then inquire as to what your last salary was. More than likely the person you're talking with will say, "I'm terribly sorry but I'm not at liberty to reveal that information." If—and this is a very big "if"—anyone does reveal your salary you'll have good cause for a lawsuit. Individuals have sued and won in such cases when they feel that their chances for substantial salary increases have been hindered as a result of the release of such information.

Why is the information so important? Why do your future employers want to know what you earned in your last job? Clearly they want to use that information when they determine what they will pay you. I said earlier that revealing past salaries could cost you hundreds of thousands of dollars. Let me explain that a bit more.

When we have a job description it will very often say "Salary: $12,000 to $18,000." Usually the sole factor in determining which end of the spectrum your offer approaches is your past salary. If you were making $11,000 in your last job you'll be offered $12,000. If you were making $17,000 on your last job you'll be offered $18,000. It's as simple as that.

Let's examine what the $6,000 per year salary discrepancy really is going to cost you. If you remained with the company for four years and never got a raise, it would cost you $24,000. If you feel that you can live on the lower salary ($12,000) but got the higher salary ($18,000) and put the $6,000 into a savings account for four years it would cost you $24,000 plus interest.

But it's unlikely that you'd work in a place for four years and not get raises. More likely your salary will improve at least 20 percent every two years. If you got that sort of salary increase having started at the bottom of the range ($12,000), by the end of four years you'll be earning $17,280. If, however, you began at the peak of the salary range ($18,000) and got those same salary increases, by the end of four years you'd be earning $25,920. At that point the difference between the two incomes has gone from $6,000 to $8,640.

If you start multiplying the difference between the two salaries plus raises over a period of twenty years, it could mean close to a half a million dollars that you're losing because someone asked you an unfair question that you felt obliged to answer. You have to think very seriously about whether or not you want to do that. While you're thinking let me add that men don't have to be told not to reveal past salaries. And men usually earn more money for the same work to boot!

It's important for you to know the salary range of any job you interview for. When an interviewer brings up the topic of money you should ask, "Just how much are you willing to pay for this position?" Generally they'll respond with a range and you can take your cue from there. If an interviewer tries to throw the ball back to you by asking, "What would you be willing to work for?" take a calculated guess at the high side of the range. START HIGH! If he asks for your last salary, you need not be specific. You can say simply that it falls in their range.

Children, Boyfriends, Husbands and Other Problems

As you can see, I'm very pragmatic about illegal questions. Let's get back to the "personal data" section of your résumé and I'll help you anticipate the kinds of questions you might be asked.

No employer is *pleased* to be hiring a woman with children. They're concerned that several times a month they'll get an early morning phone call saying that Johnny has the flu, or Susie broke her leg and "I won't be able to get to the office today." If you have children but don't want their existence to jeopardize your chance at a job, you have to deal with an employer's anxiety.

I think that the best way to do that is to raise the issue of children yourself. When an interviewer notes that you're married, you might say, "Yes, and I have two children, age nine and eleven. I've been working ever since the youngest was three and I'd like you to know that I've never missed a day's work because of either of my kids. They've got a working mother and a doting grandmother, which keeps all four of us very happy." The specific facts of that answer aren't nearly as important as the message I've conveyed. You must convince your employer that you'll be a responsible, reliable employee.

One client of ours always asks single women if they want to get married and have a family. What that interviewer is really saying is, "Are you going to get quickly married, quickly pregnant and leave us after we've spent $40,000 on training you?" If you want a job you must calm his fears. One way to do that is to answer, "First of all I'm a career woman. I have no one that I'm interested in right now, so there's no likely companion in the immediate future. But I wouldn't rule out marriage. It may happen that I'd be interested in marriage, but only with someone who respected my right to be independent. I would only marry a man who would give me equal status as a working person. If I find that sort of person, and if he interests me in other ways as well, I might get married. However, as far as children go, I think the world is already overpopulated and it needs nothing less than a contribution from me. I'm not interested in planning a family."

If, a year or two down the road, you decide to have a child, you can deal with any problems that arise from that decision then. The point of all these hypothetical situations is twofold. First, you should be able to anticipate any question that you'll be asked on an interview. If you take the time to think about those questions you're more likely to have good answers for them. Second, you must learn to get behind an interviewer's language to the essence of his question. If he asks about children, he's not interested in your innermost feelings about motherhood. *He's interested in deciding whether or not to hire you.*

Your Work History

Another area of your résumé that could cause problems in an interview is your work history. I alluded earlier to the fact that bright, ambitious women will have a tendency toward spotty work histories. If you have a real history of job jumping there's only one thing you can do.

You have to deal squarely with your interviewer and educate him about women. This is what I would say:

> *I grew up naively thinking that my goal in life was to get married and have children. But somewhere between the ages of twenty-two and twenty-four it hit me right between the eyes that I had squandered the vocational preparation time allocated to me. It just didn't occur to me to spend my college years preparing for a real career.*
>
> *So I got a job right out of school doing clerical work for someone who wasn't as intelligent as I am. The work was boring, I wasn't making any money, and I didn't think there was any point in staying there until they made me president of the company.*
>
> *Every time I left a job I didn't leave it because I was going somewhere else. I left it because I was running away from something. I suppose I was hoping that someone would discover my intelligence and talent and utilize me.*
>
> *Then I met someone in sales. I'm dying to have a stable career, but it's hard to be stable when you're sitting behind a typewriter making $150 a week. This is my opportunity to realize my talents, and you don't have to be worried about my running* away. *I'm all too happy to have a place to run* toward.

Obviously you needn't use my words. You have to sound like yourself, and you have to convey your seriousness of purpose.

Another problem that can arise when an interviewer looks at your work history involves accounting for gaps. Let's say you have a gap of two months between jobs. The fact of the matter may be that you spent that time pounding the pavement looking for a job. Maybe you were considered but not hired by ten different companies. If that's the case, you wouldn't want to share that information with the interviewer. Why should you suggest to him that anyone has ever had even a moment's reservation about hiring you?

You also wouldn't want to tell the interviewer that you decided to take it easy for two months. That information might suggest that you're lazy and prefer not working. Ideally, you should give the interviewer the impression that you're a work-a-holic.

You might do well to say that you took the two months between jobs to travel. You might even say that you knew once you found yourself professionally you would never again have the opportunity to travel for a big chunk of time and decided to seize the opportunity. With that sort of answer you're indicating that you don't plan to take two months off every year to travel, that you tend to get lost in your work, and that you're capable of planning ahead and making the most of every situation.

Another question that's likely to come up when an interviewer discusses your job history is, "Why did you leave this job?" You're only allowed to say that you left *one* job because of a personality conflict. Only one. And the one time that you say it you really have to come down hard on the other person and build yourself up. You can explain that you've never had that sort of conflict before and that if they were to call up the company to speak with your former boss they'd probably discover that he was no longer there . . . that he'd been brutally murdered.

My intention is not to convince you to misrepresent yourself, but I don't want you to do yourself any damage either. I call it the slice of bread vs. the loaf of bread problem. A loaf of bread may look terrific, but when it's all sliced you may find one piece with some flaw. That flaw doesn't mean the rest of the loaf wasn't terrific. You can still have enjoyed the bread, even with its flaw. But chances are you wouldn't have bought the loaf if you'd seen the flaw from the onset.

When a woman applies for a job she presents herself to an interviewer as a loaf of bread. If you think you're an attractive loaf of bread—a good employment risk—you may not see anything wrong with laying all your slices on the table. "What's wrong with telling the truth," you may ask, "since I'm a desirable package?"

The answer is that the interviewer doesn't really know you. He doesn't know what a good loaf of bread you are yet. He only gets to see slices of your personality. He is dealing only with an impression of you, and his impression is still changing, still forming, every time you reveal another slice. And to make matters worse, his impressions are totally subjective, based on his subjective impressions of hundreds of other applicants. His conclusions regarding your future don't necessarily have to be based on any substantiating data whatsoever.

As a consequence of this it's a woman's responsibility to see to it that she isn't disadvantaged in her interview. She must insure that she doesn't allow one aspect of herself—one slice of bread—to make her look like a bad loaf. She must be aware of every isolated response she makes and how it reflects on the whole picture she's presenting.

Bragging

I said earlier that you had to learn how to brag *nicely* on your résumé. Actually, bragging is more important on an interview than it is on a résumé, and you have to learn how to talk positively about yourself and still maintain credibility. The best way to do that is to use third-person references.

Let's assume that someone asks you why you think you'd

be good in sales. That question, by the way, is certain to come up on any sales interview, and you'd do well to be ready with an answer. Rather than saying, "I'm a born persuader," you'd do well to say, "For as long as I can remember people have told me that I'm a born persuader."

It's important to get a lot of positive information about yourself into an interview, and we all have a hard time listening to someone who spends an hour talking about how terrific they think they are. If you discuss how other people see you you're suggesting some objective point of view. If you want to include one real zinger that will indicate self-confidence and independence you can always say, "I believe in myself. I know that if there's something I really want to do, I'll work at it until I'm successful."

Games Interviewers Play

Strengths and Weaknesses

Very often an interviewer will ask you to discuss your greatest strengths. That's a nice question because it gives you an opportunity to score points. And that's the time to start talking about how people have always said you're a great persuader; how your brother-in-law told you ten minutes after he met you that you're an easy person to feel close to; that the local checkout person at your supermarket said that before she even knew you she would have cashed your checks because you just seem like the kind of person she could trust, etc.

After you've discussed your high points for a while the interviewer will look you in the eyes and say, "Now tell me what you consider to be your greatest weaknesses." Something about the way he's asked the question makes you feel like you'll score points if you *really* tell him something awful about yourself. In fact, you may even feel that the more awful the confidence is, the more impressed he'll be with your honesty, and the more likely it is that he'll hire you.

There is something nice about that idea, but unfortunately it has nothing to do with the reality of interviewing and hiring. You may not realize it, but that sort of interpretation is a feminine interpretation. Many women will come right out and say, "Well, people are often put off by the fact that I talk so much," or "Try as I may I never seem to get anywhere on time."

That sort of answer may give you a clear conscience, but it will never get you a job. The purpose of an interview is to get a job offer. You've heard that a dozen times before, but you have to really drill the message into your head. Every answer that you give should be slanted so that you'll get an offer. Now think about some "bad faults" that a potential employer might consider to be positive.

You might say, "I'm a terrible work-a-holic. I tend to get so caught up in work that I don't leave room for other things." That trait might be considered awful by your boyfriend, but an employer will read that as positive. You might also say that you tend to be compulsive. That deep inside of you you feel that there's a right and a wrong way to do things and that you just can't rest until you know things are right. Another "good bad" trait might be that you get overinvolved with people. You just can't help but get involved. When you meet a person and hear about their problems you can't step aside and say, "Look, that's their problem, not mine."

Reread the section on what makes a successful salesperson, and then devise "bad" traits that will emphasize what a good saleswoman you'll be. An interviewer doesn't want to hire someone unless he's convinced that she's the best candidate for the job, and it's up to you to do the convincing.

The Discouraging Game

Frequently about halfway through an interview the interviewer will say, "Look, I think you're terrific. In fact, you're too terrific for this job. You look too fashionable . . . too chic . . . for the nitty gritty of what you'll be doing. We need someone who'll be able to open crates, climb a ladder, stack a shelf. It's dirty work and I just don't see you doing dirty work."

If you weren't given any of the "dirty work" information before you scheduled your interview, you might be surprised. You might think, the guy is right. I am too fashionable to spend my days opening crates and stacking shelves. As soon as you agree with him you've not only lost yourself the job, but you've lost yourself the job *offer*. And the job *offer* is what you're there for.

If you say, "Hang on a second. I'm very energetic and very strong. I know how to climb a ladder and open a crate and I can always bring an apron to work with me if I don't want to get dirty. I want this job and if part of it involves dirty work, it's not beneath me to get a little dirty!" you're likely to be surprised at the end of the interview. No sales job is all that dirty. The interviewer is likely to say, "Oh, and by the way, if you have to do that dirty work once a year it would be a lot. We just like to check out attitudes."

Tell Me about Yourself

Another popular interview game goes like this. An interviewer will introduce himself to you, sit down and say, "You seem like a bright young woman. I'll bet that you know what I need to find out about you, so why don't you just interview yourself and I'll sit back and listen."

If you've done your homework this sort of interview should be easy. Ideally, before you go on an interview you should try to anticipate the questions you'll be asked and be prepared for them with answers. Four or five good questions should give you a solid twenty-minute interview. I'd suggest the following, although you'll have to tailor them to suit your particular background:

1. Why are you interested in sales?
2. Why do you think you'd do well in sales?
3. Why are you interested in this particular area of sales?
4. What would you like to be doing in five years?
5. How does a career fit into your private life?

When someone asks you to interview yourself, don't get into a long monologue. Talking straight for twenty minutes is difficult and you'll tend to get off the track. If you actually ask yourself questions (i.e., "Well, if I were to interview myself I think my first question would be, 'Why are you interested in sales?' and I'd say . . .") you'll find it easier to remain within a structure. Your interviewer will be judging you on the quality of your questions as well as the quality of your answers.

This preparation will also serve to answer another typical interview question: "Who is Jane Jones? Jane, I've never met you before. I'd like you to take ten or fifteen minutes to tell me about yourself."

Better than describing your childhood, your likes, dislikes, etc., which is the normal response, you can describe yourself in terms of why you are interested in sales, why you feel you'd be successful, etc. It is a much more relevant picture of you.

What Would You Do If . . . ?

Another game interviewers play involves a hypothetical situation. Usually, the situation will evoke anxiety. You'll be called upon to deal with the sort of stressful situation that might occur if you were employed as a saleswoman.

"Suppose," the interviewer will say, "that you're on your

way to a very important sales meeting. A client that you've been after for a year has finally agreed to meet with you and he's agreed to get all of the chief executives of his company to sit in on the meeting. You will be making your presentation in front of eight very important men. On your way to the client you get caught in a terrible traffic jam. If you get out of your car you'll have no place to park it. If you get into a cab it won't get you there any faster. If you get out and walk and leave your car to be towed away you'll still be forty-five minutes late. What do you do?"

In this sort of interview you can rely on the fact that your hypothetical situation will be grim beyond your imagination. Obviously you can't sit in your interviewer's office and say, "I think I'd cry." You must work out an answer. And the best way to approach these problems is to *really* try and think about what you'd do. You can't be cute.

The important thing for you to remember when you try to work your way out of a hypothetical stress situation is that there is no one correct answer. You may devise one solution, the next candidate another, and you may both do very well on the test. Use your head. And just do the best you can.

Sell Me That Lamp

Frequently an interviewer will point to something in his office and say, "Sell me that." The interviewer's goal, in such instances, is to see you in action. Since I believe that you can't sell someone something that you know nothing about, my response to that request would be to say, "I'd like to sell you something, but I think it's important to know your product before you sell it. Since I know nothing about that lamp would you mind if I sell you . . ." Then you can sell your interviewer a product that you've been selling in your last job, or you can sell him on jogging, tennis, or something about which you feel enthusiastic.

If an interviewer is persistent and says, "No. I want you to sell me that lamp," you can turn to him and say, "Okay. But before I sell it to you I have to have some information." Then ask him everything you can think of about the lamp. Is it new or is it an antique? How many colors does it come in? Does it have a warranty? Is it mechanically perfect? How much does it cost? How long will you have to wait for delivery?

When you can't think of another question about the lamp you can turn to your interviewer and say, "Now, Mr. Jones, let me tell you about a terrific lamp." Then you give him back all the information he gave you, and at the end of your sales presentation you can say, "Now tell me what you think. Are you interested in the lamp?" Probably he'll say, "Well, let me think it over. I'll give you a call when I make my decision." In order to show that you want to retain the sales initiative you can say, "Fine. But I'm in and out of my office, so just in case I miss you, I'll get back to you." And that's the end.

The Stress Tests

Many interviewers think it's important to see how a job candidate responds to stress and will structure the entire interview in such a way as to create stress. In such situations interviewers might be nasty ("You don't look to me like someone who can sell"). They may ask questions that have no good answer like, "If you met me in a bar would you go out with me?" If you say yes, they'll be concerned about your ability to handle sexual come-ons. If you say no, they'll be insulted.

The most important thing to remember if you find yourself in that sort of interview is that the interviewer is *playing a game*. He doesn't really dislike you. He won't really be hurt. If you allow your real feelings to come into play you're not likely to perform well. If you can step outside of your feelings for the time being and concentrate on how to win the game, you'll be able to talk with your head.

You might say, "Well, I'm married so I wouldn't be interested in going out with anyone. When I wasn't married I didn't go to bars. They don't seem like good meeting places to me. But given those two facts I'd have to say that if I met you in a bar I'd want to talk with you for a while and get to know you. I never went out with men on a strictly appearance basis, and if I liked you after we'd talked a while I'd certainly be open to dating you."

As to the first point about not looking for someone who could sell, you might say that appearances aren't always what they seem. The important thing is not to engage in an emotional battle with your interviewer. The goal is to get the job offer—not to win a friend.

Psychological Testing

There are certain corporations that require their salespeople to go through a battery of psychological testing before they do any hiring. By the time you've finished reading this book you should have a very clear idea of what makes a good saleswoman. If you want to get a job you'll take any tests with those prerequisites in mind. Don't worry about opening up your psyche in the corporation. Worry about getting the job.

The Eating Interview

It's likely that your second or third interview might be scheduled for lunch. The rules for an "eating" interview are very much the same as for any other interview. You are going to do most of the talking, so order something that is simple to eat with the lowest number of potential hazards. If you feel like ordering duck, resist the temptation.

Follow-Up

Your work isn't finished when you get home after an interview. After every interview you must write a thank-you letter. I'm not sure why people who interview thousands of applicants every year want to receive thousands of thank-you letters, but I do know that it's very important.

I've actually heard clients say that "Jane Jones got the job instead of Betty Smith because Betty Smith didn't have a good follow-through."

Over the years I've discovered that "good follow-through" means a simple thank-you note. I'd suggest something like this:

Dear Mr. White:

I just want to thank you for your time and to reiterate how excited I am about the possibility of selling Birmingham paper.

I hope to hear from you soon.

Sincerely,

If you have nice handwriting, write the letter out in longhand. If your penmanship is illegible, type it. The important message to get across is that YOU WANT THE JOB!

PART
3

How to Sell

CHAPTER

8

The
Sales Presentation

Everything I know about sales I learned from watching women sell, and most of the women I watched were never trained by anyone but themselves. I discovered what they had discovered: selling came "naturally." The women who did it best had, in effect, been doing it all their lives. They had been *teaching, explaining, persuading* without ever thinking it was "selling." They had been doing it with enthusiasm, with conviction, with humor, with their total personalities, and the most effective persuaders were those blessed with an abundance of wit, charm, intelligence . . . or whatever that combination of qualities is that people have forever been describing as "the born salesman."

In 1967, when I still thought I was training saleswomen rather than learning from them, I was continually amazed at how often one of my trainees would deliver what I considered a mistake-ridden sales presentation and still get the sale. Then

I began to understand the relationship between *what* was said and *who* said it; I began to realize that the *atmosphere* of the sales presentation was as important as the *message* of the sales presentation, that the music was indeed as important as the words.

And these women did it "naturally."

Every day of your life you're explaining your attitudes, your beliefs, and your preferences to other people. When you get someone to do what you want, haven't you made a sale? When you change someone's mind, isn't that the same thing?

When we gave men the authoritarian role in our society's basic social unit (the family), they were able to develop into strong, silent, monosyllabic types without any seeming disadvantage. You don't have to be verbal when you're the boss. Being loud was more important than being articulate.

Now with the emerging new social values, in a relationship that is supposed to be equal, loud counts for nothing. The ability to reason and articulate is the new value, and the power of persuasion is the name of the new game.

Guess who's been practicing?

The world is not made up of right and wrong; it's made up of persuaders and persuadees. If a man and wife are deciding whether or not the new car should be a convertible, whether the new home should have a swimming pool or a tennis court, where to go for a vacation, or what to watch on television, the "best decision" will usually be the persuadee agreeing to do what the persuader wanted to do.

What a woman does in the business world is not alien to what she has been doing in the home or the classroom. There is less to learn than she realizes.

I have a friend who was offered his first district manager's job, but it required that he relocate to North Dakota. When he talked to me, he said he would love to grab it but it would be a waste of time to even mention it to his wife. I asked him why his wife didn't want to relocate, and he said, "Oh, she'd relocate, but not to North Dakota."

I asked my friend what he knew about North Dakota. He said, "Nothing."

I asked him what his wife knew and again he said, "Nothing." I then asked why he thought she wouldn't move there and he said, "Would you?"

My friend, in his ignorance of North Dakota, was about to persuade his wife to not do something he wanted her to do. He would have started off with, "You wouldn't be interested in moving to North Dakota, would you?" And she would have quickly said, "God, no!" She would have said "No" because his own attitude, tone of voice, look and phraseology would have persuaded her to say "No."

I told him to say, "How would you like to relocate to a place like Denver?" Now Denver has a lot of enthusiasts. They have Bronco-mania for the football team, great skiing, fresh air, backpacking in the mountains and a generally positive attitude toward the outdoor life. And as soon as his wife gave a positive response or a show of interest he should say, "It's a place better than Denver. It's in North Dakota and it's the way Denver and Taos, New Mexico, *used* to be before so many people started locating there. It has skiing, good schools and a healthy, outdoor life-style." Etc., etc.

My mother was never a saleswoman, but she had an uncanny instinct for persuasion. When I was a child, whenever I had to ask my father for permission to do something or buy something, I would run outside to meet his car in the driveway and make the request before he even turned the motor off. After many tearful rejections, my mother took me aside and said, "Wait until after dinner. When he comes home from work he's tired, he's tense; let him relax. Let him have dinner, *then* ask for what you want."

My sales results improved dramatically. The psychology of persuasion exists everywhere.

Saleswoman Wanted: Must Have Experience

In six years, and after working with almost 1,000 clients, I've noticed something very interesting: when a client wants an *experienced* saleswoman, he never asks her what sales *theories* she believes in or what sales *approaches* or *techniques* she subscribes to. He merely wants her to have been successful in sales. There is no such thing as a sales test to determine if she knows how to sell. And there never will be. In many professions there is a proficiency test either designed or required (Legal, Accounting, Medicine, etc.) to measure what you know. In sales, the implication is that you either know how to sell or you don't; you'll either make it or you won't; it's not something someone teaches you, it's something that *doing* teaches you.

Or to put it in a sentence: HAVING SOLD SUCCESSFULLY IS SUFFICIENT PROOF THAT YOU KNOW HOW TO SELL.

And you've already been doing that.

If you're going to be successful in sales, you've already been successful. THERE'S NO SUCH THING AS AN INEXPERIENCED SALESWOMAN. A potential saleswoman has already been selling without ever realizing the market value of those special skills.

Selling Is Common Sense—Naturally

There are only three parts to a sales presentation: *What* you say (How to Construct a Sales Presentation), *How* to say it (How to Give a Sales Presentation), and *How to find out whether or not it worked* (How to Close).

Here's a simple test to guide you in the formulation of a sales presentation. It's not intentionally simple. It's simple because it has not been intentionally complicated in order to make it seem complicated.

1. What is a sales presentation?
   ANSWER: It's what a salesperson says to someone in order to sell something.
2. What is the objective of a sales presentation?
   ANSWER: To sell something.
3. How long should a sales presentation be?
   ANSWER: As long as necessary to sell the product, and no longer than is necessary.
4. What should be included in a sales presentation?
   ANSWER: Whatever is necessary to sell the product.
5. How can you tell whether or not you have a good sales presentation?
   ANSWER: When you are selling the product, you have a good sales presentation. If you are not selling the product, the problem could be:
   a. The product
   b. The sales presentation
   c. You

Now let's look at a traditional sales presentation and see why it doesn't work as well as it used to.

An office equipment salesman sits across from a prospect and immediately opens a large black book with acetate pages, an album called a sales presentation book. On page 1 is the question: "Is time money?" At the same time that the salesman opens to page 1, he says, "Mr. Jones, the one thing common to all businesses large or small is that time is money. Would you agree to that?" As the prospect agrees, the salesman turns to page 2, which says, "But money is harder to waste." The salesman says, "Money is harder to waste, however, because most businessmen have controls over their money—someone such as the accountant, or the manager, or the owner is keeping an eagle eye on the money, but who's watching time?"

Page 3 says, "Most companies can't afford efficiency experts," and the salesman supplements the message by adding, "Most companies can't afford efficiency experts, so the only alternative is to make the same person who is watching the money, watch time also. Do you think that's possible?" The prospect may say something such as "I guess so," and the salesman would add, "But you would agree it's harder, wouldn't you, Mr. Jones?"

The salesman will then turn one page after another to establish the points that efficient businesses are usually profitable ones (page 4), that all businesses must make maximum use of employee time or they will be wasting employee wages (page 5), and step by step (pages 6 to 12) the prospect will be led to the conclusion that it is more profitable to invest in a copying machine than it is to keep running around the corner to the commercial copier.

If the prospect balks by saying he doesn't think he can afford his own machine, page 13 says, "If time is money, can you afford not to own your own copier?"

If the prospect says he would like to think about it, the salesman will look a little surprised or a little disappointed but will also say something such as, "What we really have to think about is this question [Page 1 again]: 'Is time money?' " The psychology of this selling situation is one of subtle entrapment, whereby the prospect agrees little by little to the conclusion that the only solution to his problem is to buy the product.

The concepts of selling by deductive reasoning, "staying on the track," and using reinforced visual aids to hold the attention of the prospect begin to lose their effectiveness in a direct ratio to the sophistication of the prospect. If the prospect has never *seen* such a presentation before, he is much more likely to be swayed and persuaded than if he had seen ten such presentations.

But if he *has* seen ten similar presentations, he will be a reluctant prospect. He will watch for fallacious reasoning in the deductions. He will be looking for his escape *before* he gets to page 13.

The very *familiarity* of this presentation becomes a disadvantage; the *process* of selling the product has become the problem.

I have been asked by more than fifty major corporations to review their sales presentations and to determine if the language or approach would be unsuitable for the female salespeople that have been added to their staffs. In each instance I have requested the opportunity to also question the top-performing saleswoman on the staff. Consistently, I explain to the women what my function is as an outside consultant and that I will treat anything they tell me with confidentiality, but that I am talking to them because they are successful and it is the corporation's intent to try to improve the performance of the other women on the staff, etc., etc. And when I casually ask, "How closely do you follow the sales presentation?" WITHOUT EXCEPTION I HAVE HEARD ONLY A SLIGHT VARIATION OF THE FOLLOWING ANSWER: "Not too closely." The answer is almost apologetic until I ask, "What do you do?" Then these successful saleswomen explain, "Well, the first thing I do is try to make the prospect comfortable, kind of relax him. Many of the prospects don't expect a woman or they're more curious about me than they are about the product at first, so I have to get beyond that so they'll pay attention when I start talking about the product. And then . . . I guess I just kind of talk about the product. I mean I don't leave out anything that's important, but I just do it a different way. I guess more like discussing it rather than doing it exactly the way they want me to do it. But anyway, they still buy it!" When I ask the women why they don't follow the presentation, they usually respond, "Well, I follow it . . . kind of . . . I just put it in my own words and do it my own way. I just think it's better that way."

How to Construct a Sales Presentation

It's very important that you learn how to construct a sales presentation. There are very specific things that must be included when you present your product to a prospect, and unless you're aware of exactly what those things are, you won't be able to do a good job.

The most important outgrowth of being very well prepared—of learning how to construct a good sales presentation—is that you'll be able to improvise and talk in a relaxed way. The better you prepare, the less canned you're likely to sound.

What should be included in a sales presentation? Whatever is necessary to sell the product. What's necessary?

1. A description of the product or service. (Product Description)
2. Why someone would want to buy it. (Benefits)
3. Why someone *might* not want to buy it. (Objections)
4. What someone might buy instead. (Competition)
5. Any other information required to answer a prospect's objections. (Other Information)

That's all.

The first step is to collect and list all data under these five headings. It doesn't matter what the product or service is, it is exactly the same process for automobiles or typewriters. This is the skeleton for everything that could ever be sold.

Let's sell a membership to your local "Y." What would someone want to know about membership privileges?

Product Description
1. Price is $140 per year.
2. Facilities include a pool, running

track, basketball
courts, weight room,
etc., etc.
3. Towels are not
included.
4. Hours of operation.
5. Location.
6. Guest privileges.

You would collect and list anything and everything that you might presume a prospect would be interested in. Then you move to two:

Benefits
1. Health
2. Cheap
3. Cosmetic

After benefits, you list every possible reason you can conceive that someone might raise for not wanting a membership:

Objections
1. Don't have time.
2. Too crowded.
3. No tennis courts.
4. Exercise makes me
hungry.
5. Belonged once
and never used it.
6. Etc., etc.

Then competition:

Competition
1. Other health clubs.
2. Prefers jogging.
3. Plays tennis.
4. Plays golf.
5. Etc., etc.

Other Information would be information required to answer such objections as "I've never heard of your company before," or "How can I be sure your product is as good as you say it is?" In these instances, the saleswoman would realize that she must have a history of her company, or a list of satisfied clients, or testimonials, or research reports. Anything available that would answer the objection.

Once you have collected the basic data, the presentation itself is created with the following guidelines:

1. Describe the product as if the prospect will ask, "What is your product and why should I buy it?"

2. Plan to answer anticipated objections before they are raised; and the bigger the objection is, the sooner your presentation should answer it.

3. Determine what information you will want to get from your prospect *before* you begin your presentation.

4. A good presentation should be easy to remember and comfortable to say.

5. The presentation should be flexible in form and length.

6. It must not sound "canned."

7. Determine what language you will use to find out whether or not your prospect is going to buy your product.

8. Use every justifiable superlative you can get into your presentation.

9. You should have the answer for every objection that your prospect could raise.

10. Don't be afraid to use yourself as an authority.

The easiest format to begin working with in constructing a presentation is to pretend that as soon as you walk into your prospect's office he will ask, "What is your product and why should I buy it?" It's not a difficult pretense because that is the same question that all buyers ask all sellers, whether they phrase it that way or whether they even verbalize it. The answer to the question is then necessarily a *description of the product* commingled with its *benefits*.

If you anticipate objections that must be answered before the prospect raises them, you have two primary advantages: If the prospect has his objection answered *without* verbalizing it, he doesn't have to defend it. And, once an objection is removed, the prospect is more receptive to the selling message.

In 1973, when I was selling the benefits of hiring saleswomen instead of men, I became very frustrated when so many male managers seemed fearful about taking on all the unnecessary "problems" that came with the female gender. And I quickly realized that once the manager verbalized his own attitudinal problem, no matter how unsubstantiated it was, I had a tough debate on my hands and the referee and judge was the guy I was gently arguing with. Finally I had a manager tell me that the only woman he would consider hiring had to be a cross between Marilyn Monroe and Madame Curie. Without hesitating, I said, "I have her. In fact she doesn't even menstruate." And before he could react, I explained, "She's dead, too."

He laughed, but he gave me a job order.

The next time I made a sales presentation, I told the story. The new manager laughed, *and never raised the objection.*

From then on, my basic sales presentation became a series of funny little stories about how managers "used to" have hang-ups about hiring women. I actually believe that half the women I placed in 1974 were through managers who decided it was better to *hear* a funny story than to *be* one.

The importance of determining what information you want before you begin your presentation will vary from product to product, but regardless of the product, it is a key point to remember. When one of our Careers For Women saleswomen calls on a new prospect, she knows she must always ask three questions before she begins her presentation: (1) How large is your sales force? (2) Are there any women? (3) How are the women performing in relation to the other sales-people? Inevitably, we hear that the women are at the top of the sales ladder. If a manager had had only negative experiences, we would have to explain that that was extremely atypical. If the manager believes that his bad experience is *typical,* he would not listen to our list of "benefits." It was a lesson learned hard.

I made a call with a saleswoman in Philadelphia to sell a corporate program when we were presenting the Evelyn Wood Speed Reading Course to companies in the Pennsylvania area. She made a very nice presentation, concluding with, "Well, Mr. Jones, tell me what you think about our program." And he answered, "My brother took this course six months ago and he said it was the greatest waste of time and money he'd ever experienced."

That was the last time she ever gave a presentation without asking, "Mr. Jones, have you ever known anyone who has taken the Evelyn Wood Speed Reading Course? Yes, and what did he say about it?" Whether the answer was positive or negative, the time to have that information is *before* the presentation begins.

The next points, "easy to remember," "comfortable to say," "flexible," "uncanned," are the requisites for being able "to talk about your product." A presentation is live, not taped. If you want to sound like a tape, you should send the prospect a tape.

At the end of your presentation, all sales books advise you to "ask for the order," yet I've never discovered either a salesperson or a sales manager who has ever said, "And finally, Mr. Jones, may I have your order?" I once asked Lou Costello for his autograph when I was nine years old and he said, "Not now, kid." I don't know when Mr. Costello anticipated running into me again, but I remember a feeling of embarrassment from the experience, and I vowed I would never ask for an order (autograph) again.

Everyone must discover comfortable language to use when the answer to "What is your product and why should I buy it?" has been given. As much as I hated hearing the bad news, if I hadn't said anything, I would have invested more of my time in wasted effort.

I don't believe you should sell anything without knowing the answer to all objections. You may disagree with your prospect, you may not be able to change your prospect's attitude, but if you honestly feel that there is an unanswerable objection and that your only plan is to talk fast and pray to God that the prospect buys before he balks, then I suggest that you begin looking for another product to sell.

The last two points can be illustrated by retelling a single eye-opening experience that happened in 1968 when I was a vice-president of the Evelyn Wood organization. We were marketing to schools and colleges throughout the United States, and the academic community was properly suspicious of our claims that "Our average student reads 4.7 times faster with equal or better comprehension." As a testimonial to our authenticity, we loudly and frequently announced that 300,000 graduates were walking around in the midst of the slower reading population, that some forty Senators and/or Congressmen had taken the program and recommended it (names withheld to protect the innocent), that it had been taught on more than 85 college campuses, etc., etc.

One day I stopped into a fashionable men's store named J. Press on East 44th Street in New York. I had wanted to buy a pair of summer slacks.

I am not a picky shopper, merely an indecisive one. I had tried on several pair of pants and was standing in front of a three-way mirror, rotating myself in first one direction, then the other. Finally the salesman came up to me and asked what I was doing. "Oh," I replied, a little self-conscious at the amount of time I was taking making up my mind, "I can't stand slacks that wrinkle up behind the knees after you sit down in them, and I was just checking these out." He watched me turn and gesture to the suspicious area, and then he said, "Those pants you have on right now, that particular combination of Dacron and worsted is the most wrinkle-resistant fabric ever made."

I bought four pair.

I was walking back to my office on Fifth Avenue, mulling over the headline: "More corporate presidents have taken the Evelyn . . ." when I realized I had just bought four pair of slacks because a guy I never saw before said, "Those pants that you have on right now, that particular combination of Dacron and worsted is the most wrinkle-resistant fabric ever made." I didn't demand to see some testimonial! I didn't want a research paper from the wool bureau! *He* said they were the best and I bought four pair.

He was the authority. He was the expert.

When you are selling, you are too. If you believe in your product, get the word "absolutely" into your sales presentation. Be definite, not tentative. When your prospect, your friend, asks, "Are you really sure this thing's gonna do all it's supposed to do?" if your answer is "I think so," you need more product knowledge; if your answer is "I hope so," you need a new product; if your answer is "Absolutely," you've helped someone make a buying decision.

Before I get into the mechanics of a sales presentation— its preparation and delivery—I want to remind you again of how much "natural know-how" you're starting out with. If you went out *cold* and improvised your way through a month's worth of sales presentations you'd probably arrive at the same conclusions that I did, and you'd probably find a comfortable, successful style.

Unfortunately, very few of you have quite the same faith

in your instincts that I do. The same woman who can persuade a group of eight to eat Mexican food will walk into her first sales meeting oblivious of her own power. She'll forget the connection between last night's Mexican dinner and the business at hand. And *that's* the point of this chapter. I want to emphasize the connection between the sales presentation and your own experience, and save you the time of discovery.

There's something about the label SALES PRESENTATION that implies some sort of mystical technique, and if you think about your sales presentations as Sales Presentations you're likely to panic. Can I do that? Can I do that thing called a Sales Presentation? Well, I know that the best way for you to approach your first presentations is to stop thinking of them with their label on. You have to move from the unfamiliar label to familiar ground.

Remember the woman I accompanied on a sales call who began discussing gourmet Chinese cooking with her client? When we left her prospect's office she was annoyed with me for fidgeting during her presentation. I learned that the presentation didn't begin when she started to talk about her product. It began when she established a comfortable environment for the presentation of her product. She walked into the office and looked around. As soon as she found what she was looking for —familiar ground—she felt that she knew what she was doing.

"Chinese cooking" served as a transitional object for those two people. As soon as the saleswoman began to discuss something familiar she understood—in an almost organic way— that her sales presentation was an integral part of her life. She took the label off what she was doing and did it better!

I don't mean to suggest that a good sales presentation consists of a half hour of shooting the breeze. Your job is to sell, and no one is going to buy your product because you're interested in Chinese cooking. Ultimately you'll have to communicate enough information about your product so that your client can determine whether or not it's something that he needs. The important aspect of establishing familiar ground is that it makes *both* you and your client feel more comfortable. Feeling comfortable will make it easier for you to present your product and easier for your client to listen.

Before we discuss how to give a sales presentation, it is important to acquaint ourselves with the person who will be hearing it: our prospect.

And who is our prospect? He is you. He is me. They are us.

It is a common mistake in sales to visualize the seller as a real person and the prospect as a thing.

Unfortunately, any strategy designed to appeal to a thing rarely appeals to a person.

In sales, if we are salespeople, we are both buyers and sellers. Consequently, if we want to know and understand our prospect, we need only analyze and understand ourselves. Every salesperson should make a list of those things that would please and annoy them as buyers. This is my list:

Please	Annoy
Respect for my time	Being rushed
Not being talked down to	Being talked to like a robot
Not being tricked,	Not being listened to
etc.	Being pressured,
	etc.

The best advice for any salesperson is NEVER FORGET THAT *YOU* ARE THE PROSPECT. If your approach or your manner or your strategy would annoy you, it will annoy your prospect. Presume that the prospect will respond to the same things you would respond to:

Honesty rather than chicanery.
Clarity rather than confusion.

Friendliness rather than intimidation.
A relaxed atmosphere rather than pressure.

The format for giving a sales presentation consists of four parts:

1. Small talk or social talk.
2. "Qualifying" the prospect.
3. The sales presentation itself.
4. The close.

And these are tips on how to give it:

First, don't think of selling, think of creating a situation that makes it easy to buy. This attitude will give you the proper tone of voice and will result in a logical, honest, straightforward sales presentation.

If you think you're "selling," you risk looking, talking, and acting like a salesman. And salesmen alert and alarm buyers.

When I first moved to Pennsylvania, I bought a house, and like most homeowners I wanted to have a nice lawn. I didn't know much about fixing a lawn so I called a service called Lawn-a-mat and they sent one of their representatives to my house.

As we walked on my crabgrass he told me what his service would do. They'd get rid of the bad grass, plant some good grass, take care of it, and keep my house from being the shame of the neighborhood. It all sounded fine to me. He went on to say what it would cost for me to have Lawn-a-mat, and although it was expensive I was ready to sign on the dotted line.

We talked a bit more about my lawn and the sort of care it would need, and the more we talked the more I felt that this representative really understood lawns and the particular needs of my lawn. I said, quite casually, that all of this was new to me. I explained that I'd recently come from California and that there wasn't much involved with having a good lawn out there. We didn't have the snow and ice and frozen ground that was part of a Pennsylvania winter.

At that point the Lawn-a-mat man turned to me and said, "I don't think you're really right. We have Lawn-a-mat franchises all over the country and our statistics indicate that the franchises in California do just as well as the franchises on the East Coast."

And at *that* point I got turned off Lawn-a-mat. The representative had interrupted his sales presentation to remind me that he was a salesman. He stopped being a "Lawn-a-mat expert" and started being a salesman as soon as he began discussing his "business." And that set off an alarm in my head and prevented me from buying his service!

Having a nice smile, an infectious laugh, are sales assets; sounding like a record is an alarm.

Next, always create a situation for your prospect to talk *before* you begin your sales presentation. If small talk is developed, it should go on as long as the prospect is enjoying it. It should not be forced. If the prospect declines or seems disinterested in small talk, the saleswoman should proceed immediately to the qualification of the prospect. The first goal of the qualifying step is to get the information that the saleswoman had predetermined to be important before beginning the actual production. ("Have you or anyone you know ever taken the Evelyn Wood Speed Reading Course?")

In addition to gathering essential information, there are several important additional advantages:

1. If your prospect is talking, you have an opportunity to size him up and determine his personality. Is he friendly? Mild? Tough? Brusque? If your prospect is a pussy cat with a hostile countenance you'll be much more relaxed with that

insight while giving your presentation than you would without it.

2. While you relax, you have the opportunity to make a good impression as an interested, friendly listener.

3. There is a psychological advantage in not having to suddenly take off your coat, shake hands, and be "on." If the prospect is talking first, you can let your adrenaline levels subside, and you and your prospect can get used to each other's face and personality. Many early points of a sales presentation are lost because the prospect is more interested in adjusting to you as a person than he is in hearing about your product.

There is an obvious advantage in establishing a relationship that is on the same social level with your prospect. Many salespeople deport themselves as either a superior or an inferior. However, neither talking down nor up to your prospect will help your cause. Have you ever wondered why the biggest business deals are closed on a golf course? Everyone would rather do business with a friend than a stranger.

One of the worst pieces of advice ever given in sales is the counsel that people like to hear their own names, so be sure to repeat the prospect's name as often as possible. The more often you repeat "No, Mr. Jones," "Yes, Mr. Jones," "Don't you agree, Mr. Jones?" the more you are strangers. He's not John, he's *Mr.* Jones. I strongly advise *against* calling a prospect Mr., Miss, Ms., or Mrs. for just that reason. It is possible to immediately develop a tone of voice that suggests friendship and familiarity without being socially presumptuous. As you establish this kind of rapport, a "Mr." is a reminder that you are not really friends.

When to proceed to a first-name basis is a matter of judgment and sensitivity. If in doubt, wait. Unfortunately, there are no fixed guidelines such as "the second call" but if you are alert, you will see positive signals when the prospect is inviting you to become a friend. Announcing himself by his first name ("This is John"), calling you by your first name ("Hello, Mary"), or using a tone of voice reserved for friends are positive signals.

Be more cautious if the prospect's age or business standing is substantially senior to your own.

In keeping with the same rationale, it is a good idea to accept tea, coffee, or a soft drink if it is offered during a business call. If you are both having coffee, the atmosphere of an office changes subtly, and your prospect is in the position of acting like a host. ("How do you take your coffee?")

Very often, when a prospect finally decides he wants to buy, he also decides he wants to buy from *you*.

The next tip is to remember that if anything ever goes wrong during your sales presentation or throws you off balance, ASK QUESTIONS.

Asking questions not only gives you time to think before you have to respond, but the additional information you gather from your questions may be the basis for your answer.

Remember the problem with the prospect who said, "My brother took this course and said it was the greatest waste of time and money he ever experienced in his life"? The saleswoman's name was Carolyn MacEwen, and even though she admitted to me later that she thought she was going to either faint or get sick, the prospect never knew it. Without hesitating a second, she asked a series of questions: Where did he take the course? Did he attend all eight lessons? Did he do the required practice? Did he apply for his refund? As soon as the prospect began saying, "I don't know, I'm not sure," Carolyn had regained the advantage.

She then politely explained that speed reading was a skill, not a secret, and if someone didn't do the required practice and attend all eight lectures, the course would truly be a waste of time and money. She promised to look into it, and then proceeded to sell the prospect a corporate program for his middle management executives. That's good selling. That's good sales *woman*ship in action.

The final tip is to remember that a sales presentation is "live." You can organize what you intend to say and you can deliver it perfectly, but you can't be sure that your prospect will always cooperate.

Before Kathy Aaronson became the Assistant Publisher and Advertising Manager of the publication *"W,"* she had already earned a reputation as a brilliant and creative saleswoman. A rival publisher once said about her grudgingly: "If sales talent were music, Kathy Aaronson would be a symphony."

When we first became friends, she had been with *"W"* six months and headed an all-female sales force that had earned immediate respect in the industry. She then hired a man who was getting off to a slow start and she asked me to do her a favor and make a sales call with him as a training consultant.

This obviously required that I take a quick cram course in how to sell *"W,"* and Kathy prepared me to call on the Director of Tourism for India. She said, "I use an approach I call 'Make 'em sick, then make 'em better.' Make them aware of a problem, then solve it for them." She told me that the problem with selling India to the *"W"* reader was that India was not the most comfortable, fun place in the world to go for a vacation, but that the *"W"* reader had the time and the money to travel without the normal constraints of the average tourist. And she did not have school-age children to restrict her travel.

Properly prepared, the salesman and I called on the Director of Tourism and gave him our presentations. At the end of the presentation, he stood up and said: "Gentlemen, I am very impressed with your publication. I would like very much to have several copies of your back issues to put in our reception area. My assistant, Mrs. Nandi, is handling our advertising, however, and if you'll come with me, I'll introduce you to her." He then walked out of his office and knocked on the door of the office adjacent to his. Immediately a woman in traditional Indian dress answered the door, and he said, "Mrs. Nandi, here are two gentlemen from Mr. Fairchild's *'W.'* Gentlemen, my assistant, Mrs. Nandi." He then shook hands with us, thanked us for our time, *and turned to walk back into his office.*

Now, I told you a sales presentation was "live." You are now watching the back of the Director of Tourism disappear. Is there anything you would like to say? Is there any advantage you would like to salvage before he disappears? If there is, cover this page with your hand and START TALKING BECAUSE HE'S ALMOST IN HIS OFFICE!

IS THERE ANYTHING YOU WANT TO SAY?

As I stood there, I heard a voice say, "Make 'em sick and make 'em better," and I said, "I don't know how many back issues I can get of our publication, but I'll do what I can." He stopped and turned to face me, and I added, "I can tell you one thing. Nothing will make them more helpful than repeating your remark that you are very impressed with our publication." He smiled and thanked me for my concern.

We then went into Mrs. Nandi's office, armed with the opinion of the Director, not quoted by us but delivered personally by him, live. One step more and we would have lost that advantage.

How to "Close"

The most confusing and misunderstood aspect of selling is what is referred to as "the close." Its precise definition is "asking for the order" or asking your prospect to buy your product.

If you ever look through classified or display ads in the "Help Wanted" section under "Sales," you will see what leads to the confusion: "Good Closer Wanted"; "Good Salesperson Wanted, must be able to close"; "Only good closers need apply."

The implication is that a "good closer" is a special kind of salesperson. I have even heard such statements as, "She not only was a great saleswoman, but she really knew how to close."

Just to orient everyone, if all the prospects say, "No," they will say the salesperson can't sell. If all the prospects say, "I want to think about it," they'll say the salesperson can't close.

There have been thousands of articles written on "How to Close." There has *never* been a sales book written that does not have a chapter or a section on "How to Close." Of all the training programs on sales that have ever been offered, the most popular subject or section is something related to "How to Close."

This has culminated in the following popular misconceptions about selling:

1. Many good salespeople don't know how to close.
2. Closing is merely a matter of language.
3. Good closers must have aggressive personalities.

The truth of the matter is, if you don't know how to close, you don't know how to sell. If you are not getting results, you'd better look at the *whole* selling situation, not just what you say at the end of your sales presentation. The problem could be:

1. You. This is usually the last place anyone looks for the problem. But selling is a very personal business. It's personal enough that you might not get sales because of the way you look, talk, act, or are.

2. The product (or service) you are selling. This is usu-

ally the first thing that gets the blame. If you are tempted to blame your product or service, ask yourself the vital question, "Is *anyone* selling it better than I am?" And, if the answer is "Yes," ask yourself the heart-stopper: "Is *everyone* selling it better than I am?" And if the answer is "Yes," you know the product or service is not to blame.

3. Your presentation. This is where you'll usually find your problem. Not in the *end* of your presentation, but in your *whole* presentation.

We originally defined "the close" as "asking for the order" or "asking your prospect to buy your product." The number one anxiety in sales is also "asking for the order" or "asking your prospect to buy your product." And the reason this is the number one anxiety is that MOST SALES PEOPLE ARE AFRAID THE ANSWER WILL BE *NO!*

And they don't want to feel rejected. And I don't blame them. When Lou Costello told me, "Not now, later," I felt rejected. I hated it.

I don't believe any good salesperson ever gets used to being rejected. That's like getting used to being beaten up.

If you don't want to be rejected, you must protect yourself from rejection.

That's my philosophy and this is how I do it:

1. You must never leave a prospect without finding out whether or not he is going to buy. There is no point in giving a sales presentation unless your goal is to make a sale. But if you can't stand rejection, NEVER ASK FOR THE ORDER UNTIL YOU ARE SURE HE IS GOING TO BUY! And that's easy to find out. When you finish your presentation, ask your prospect, "Tell me what you think." If he says, "I think this is a great product," he's telling you he wants to buy. If he says, "Well, I'm really not sure," he's telling you to keep selling. If he says, "I don't think it's right for my com-

pany," he may have legitimate reasons for not buying. In any of these examples, he did not say what you were afraid he'd say, "I don't want to buy BECAUSE I HATE YOU!"

If you're selling magazine advertising space and he says, "I think you have great editorials," you can confidently say, "Is it great enough to give us a six-time schedule?" No matter what he says, you'll get signals as to how close he is to buying. Don't ask for the order without getting positive signals. Why embarrass both of you?

2. Never give a sales presentation without knowing your closing statement. If you're going to say, "Well, now you know as much about my product as I do. Tell me what you think," use it. That's your "close."

3. No matter what he says, keep the door open. "Close" implies "end." "Open" implies "tomorrow is another day."

4. If he says "No," ask "Why?" He could be saying "No" because he misunderstood you. He could say "No" because of a problem you can solve, either immediately or at a later date. If you don't know "why," you have no chance to make the sale.

5. Reduce the vague to the specific. If your prospect says: "Let me think about it," or "It sounds interesting; let me talk to some people and I'll give you a call," *always* say, "Fine," and then be sure to tactfully probe for the problem. You can't say, "Fine, what's the problem?" but at some point before you are making your exit, you can say something such as, "If you're having budget problems, it might be possible to work our order and delivery around your fiscal period." More often than not the prospect will feel obliged to state what the problem actually is. "It's really not money, but there are two other people who ought to be consulted at this point so that we don't step on any toes."

6. Accept the inferred offer. If you are selling advertising space and the prospect asks, "Do you have any covers available?" you should get back to him with, "We're in luck. I can get you an inside front cover or an inside back cover.

Which one would you like?" (If he didn't want a cover, why would he ask if you have any available? He's not taking a survey.)

7. After you've made the sale and left his office, don't suddenly reenter unexpectedly to retrieve a glove or an umbrella. If the prospect isn't expecting you, you could create a sense of embarrassment if his back is to the door and he is talking about something he doesn't want you to hear.

And that's it. That's all. The rest is *you*.

9

How to Get Appointments

Knowing how to give a great sales presentation to your pet poodle isn't going to count for much when it's time to pay the rent. All the skill in the world won't result in a sale unless you can get in front of a prospect. No one—male or female—can succeed in sales unless she can get appointments, and getting appointments involves a good deal more than calling up a prospect and saying, "Let's get together."

Getting an appointment is actually convincing a prospect that seeing you will be a worthwhile use of his time. You may be confident that everyone you call will benefit from meeting with you, but unless you can convey that to your prospects they're going to assume that you, like the other fifteen salespeople they've spoken to that week, are going to waste their valuable time.

How do you avoid being categorized with all those other salesmen? How do you improve your chances for success? The first thing you need to do is to not sound like a typical salesman, and as a woman you're starting with an edge. No prospects are as accustomed to being called on by a woman as by a man. Yet even with the difference in gender you must watch your *tone*.

If your tone is in any way reminiscent of a salesman's tone, you'll be treated like one of the vast army of salesmen. The alarm will go off. The red flag will go up. And your path to the prospect will become loaded with obstacles.

What's the Problem?

Remember, prospects are people who like and dislike pretty much the same things that you and I do. The best way to approach these *people* is to put yourself in their place.

If you were a prospect, there would be a certain number of salespeople you would want to see and others you would want to avoid as a waste of your time. You would do your best to make this determination *before* you agreed to an appointment.

Also, since most of us feel guilty about saying "No," it would be ideal if all the "Nos" could be said through an intermediary.

Finally, there are a number of products or services that might well warrant a closer inspection, but the salesperson's personality discourages any interest. We don't like spending social time *or* business time with people we don't like.

Before you make your first call for an appointment ask yourself, "If ten people a day were calling me for an appointment, what would I want to hear?" Let's examine the most common mistakes so that you can avoid them. I'm a great believer in preventive medicine.

Repeat Calling

Consider the following scenario.

You call a prospect and his secretary picks up the phone.

She tells you that her boss isn't in and asks if you'd care to leave your name and number so that he can get back to you. You give her the information she's requested and keep yourself busy for the next hour and a half while you await his return phone call.

After a more-than-reasonable period of time you decide to give it another try. You call the same prospect, get the same secretary who says the same thing, and you leave the same name and number. Once again time passes with no return call, so you decide to try again.

Believe it or not, there are salesmen who go through this routine twenty times. By the fifth call the secretary has an edge to her voice. By the sixth call you're feeling like slamming the receiver down on your prospect's knuckles. By the tenth call you're taking great, self-righteous pleasure in the fact that your client hasn't yet gotten back to you. By the fifteenth call the secretary is considering the possibility of hiring someone to answer her phone. If you should, at some point after call number fifteen, get your client on the phone, the last thing in the world you feel like discussing with him is your product. A bit of name-calling would feel much better.

But the fact is that after the first few calls you probably won't have to worry about what to say to your prospect. He'll never call you back. The problem with *repeat calling* is that it defines your role as that of nag. After two calls your prospect is well aware that you'd like him to return your call. He doesn't suddenly become aware of your desire on call number eighteen. On the contrary.

By the time you've completed your fifth or sixth call he might even be feeling guilty about not having returned your calls, and that guilt is an added reason *not* to get back to you. Who needs to deal with guilt? He'd much rather just have you disappear from his life and he figures that if he continues to ignore you you'll eventually go away.

Most women can relate very easily to how a prospect in that position feels. Have you ever been pursued by a man you have no interest in seeing? Perhaps you gave him your phone number at a party, went home and thought about it, and decided that you really didn't want to go out with him. Unfortunately he calls the next day. Your roommate (mother, sister, brother, daughter) follows your instructions and says that you're not in just then. So he calls the next day, and the next, and the next until he's called every day for nearly a month.

The word for that sort of behavior is *harassment*, and it isn't endearing. The important thing to keep in mind when you call to make an appointment is that your goal is TO GET AN APPOINTMENT. If you engage in *repeat calling*, your goal becomes GETTING YOUR CLIENT ON THE PHONE, and those are two very different goals.

Of course, it *is* annoying when someone doesn't return your calls. But as a saleswoman you've got to put your annoyance aside for the time being. Strange as it may seem, you must protect your prospect's psychological position rather than underline it. Don't remind him of his lack of consideration.

I always recommend that women avoid the problem of unreturned calls entirely. You should never leave your number more than once, but if your prospect doesn't return your call don't call him back with the same message. On your second call you might say to the secretary that you're going to be out for the rest of the day and thought you'd try to catch him before you leave. If you make it clear that he won't be able to reach you for a few days you won't be leaving the burden of contact on him.

That sort of message avoids the issue of guilt entirely and provides a pleasant environment from which you can begin to establish a relationship with the secretary. I'll discuss your relationship with a prospect's secretary in detail later, but it always pays to have her on your side.

Where to Start

I am absolutely convinced that given unlimited time and money, any of you can get an appointment with anyone. Don't ever forget that premise. Yet the fact that you *can* get in to see anyone doesn't mean that, in reality, you *will* get in to see everyone. In reality neither your time nor your funds are limitless, and those limits are what will determine your success at getting appointments.

You may choose not to pursue some people too assiduously if your expenditures outweigh your anticipated returns. You may find it a more profitable use of your time to see three more accesssible prospects than to pursue one who's hard to get. Determining which prospects merit your time and money depends to a certain degree on the size and quality of your account list.

Before you make your first calls it's important to examine your account list carefully. Separate your biggest accounts and put them aside for the time being. You never want to cut your teeth on your big accounts. If you should call Continental Can and they ask you three questions over the phone that you should but can't answer, you'll have created a bad impression. You might even have lost the opportunity to get an appointment with that account.

You'll also have to adjust your strategy depending upon the number of clients you have. The smaller the number of clients on your list, the more time you should put into preparing for your calls. If you worked for me and I gave you a year to bring in business on five accounts, I'd want you to plan your approach as though it were the Normandy invasion. You probably wouldn't call a single person for at least two months. With that sort of caseload you'd want to find out everything possible about the companies' backgrounds before you made your calls. You'd try to learn about the people you'd be dealing with. You'd call up salespeople who had the accounts before you.

In that sort of situation every account would be crucial because each one would count as 20 percent of your account list. If, however, I started you off with 5,000 accounts and said I wanted them all covered by the end of the year you'd have to assess your approach differently. You'd have to call ninety prospects a week to get your work done and your best bet would probably be to dive in and start dialing.

Getting Past the Secretary

Whether you have five prospects or 5,000, you'll probably always have to talk to their secretaries before you talk to them, and getting past a good secretary can be a problem. If you've ever called your doctor's office and found yourself describing your symptoms and discussing treatment with his secretary you know how frustrating it can be to get stuck on the first line of defense.

Most secretaries consider it their job to protect their bosses' time, and screening phone calls is one of their most effective methods toward that end. It may well turn out that getting to talk to the prospect directly may require selling his secretary on the idea that *her boss* needs to talk with you, but the first effort should be to work *around* her rather than *through* her.

Since all of that probably sounds a bit convoluted, consider the following concrete scenario in which a salesman attempts to contact a prospect.

> Secretary: *Good morning, ABC Company. May I help you?*
> Salesman: *Yes. May I please speak with Mr. Jones?* (Pause)
> Secretary: *Certainly. May I say who's calling?*

Salesman: *Yes. This is Mr. Smith calling.* (Pause)

Secretary: *May I ask what this is in reference to, Mr. Smith?*

Salesman: *I'm selling group life insurance and I think Mr. Jones will find what I have to say very interesting.*

Secretary: *Just one moment and I'll see if he's in.* (The secretary puts Mr. Smith on hold and he, as many other life insurance salesmen, sees his life pass before his eyes because he knows that the next voice he hears will not be that of Mr. Jones.)

Secretary: *I'm sorry to have kept you waiting but Mr. Jones isn't in at the moment. If you leave your number I'll see that he gets the message.*

The obvious problem with the above conversation is that poor Mr. Smith never got to speak with his prospect to set up an appointment. Had he altered his conversation, even slightly, he might have had more success.

I will now tell you a technique that will triple the number of prospects you talk to directly. Because it is so simple, you must do it perfectly and exactly as I describe it.

When you call a prospect, ask for him by his *full* name ("John Jones"), give your full name *before it is asked for* ("Mary Smith"), and use a tone of voice *that expects to be put through to your prospect without question.*

It should be stated thus: "May I speak to John Jones and would you tell him it's Mary Smith calling."

No more and no less.

Let's analyze why this is so effective.

Most salespeople identify themselves as salespeople by the pattern of their calls. They ask for "Mr.," which implies he's a stranger; they do not volunteer their own names, which implies their own names are not meaningful to the prospect;

and they use a tone of voice that is *hoping* they won't be questioned.

Using full names is not inappropriately familiar.

Interestingly enough, the women who use this technique have even more success with it than I. When a woman says, "This is Robin Sands. I'd like to speak with John Jones, please," secretaries seem reluctant to ask what the call is in reference to. They somehow assume, when they hear a woman's voice, that their boss will recognize the name. In fact, when a secretary says, "Mr. Jones, there's a Robin Sands on the phone for you," *he* may even be a bit confused.

There are many businessmen who either innocently or not so innocently strike up a conversation at an airport cocktail lounge or on a plane, or in any of a dozen quasi-business situations, and casually extend a business card while saying, "If I can ever help you, give me a call," or, "The next time you end up going to New York, give me a call." When his secretary says, "Mr. Jones, there's a Robin Sands on the phone," he appears to be reluctant to direct his secretary to find out who Robin Sands is and why she is calling. He just doesn't want his secretary to get the wrong impression by hearing, "He gave me his card when we were stranded together in a Chicago airport and told me to call him if I ever came to New York."

Although the above confusion may work in your favor, it's important that you never actually suggest to a secretary that you have a personal relationship with her boss. You could say, "Is John in? Would you tell him it's Jane calling." And if the secretary says, "What is this call in reference to?" you can't respond with, "Just tell him who it is and *he'll* know what it's about."

If you ever succeed in getting your prospect on the phone through trickery he won't have any interest in dealing with you. He'll probably be annoyed with you for the false impression you've created with his secretary. There's a significant difference between a secretary drawing her own conclusions from your totally appropriate business behavior, and a secretary being led to believe something other than the truth as a result of your suggestions. (Remember your "Please" and "Annoy" list.)

There's one other thing that's significantly wrong with the conversation between Mr. Smith and John Jones's secretary. Mr. Smith put himself in the position of giving an inadequate part of his presentation to the secretary and relying on her to convey it to her boss. That sort of situation is something you should always avoid.

If a secretary could sell your product as well as you could she'd probably be out there selling it and earning a good deal more than $180 a week. As things stand she has no investment in presenting your need for an appointment very sympathetically. John Jones's secretary may have gone into his office and said, "There's another life insurance salesman on the phone. Shall I tell him you're busy?" If the secretary had been working for Mr. Jones for a long time and developed some autonomy she may not have even bothered to inform her boss of the call. She may have assumed that he wasn't interested in speaking with insurance salesmen and saved him the time of a consultation.

If you follow my suggestion regarding tone of voice and language but still are asked the purpose of your call, the first effort should be to avoid giving the secretary your sales presentation. For instance, if you are a commercial real estate saleswoman, you might explain that you recognize how busy her boss is, but that you only need fifteen seconds on the phone with him for a quick question about his lease. It's easy to say that someone doesn't have fifteen *minutes* for you, but anyone would sound ridiculous swearing that her boss didn't have fifteen *seconds* to spare.

What If He's Really Not In?

It is, of course, possible that Mr. Jones might actually be out of his office when you call. If that's the case and the secretary asks for your number you should still do as I suggested earlier—say that you're going to be hard to reach and ask if she can suggest a time you're most likely to reach him.

By asking a secretary when it's easiest to reach her boss you're actually establishing an alliance. She's going to *help you out*. At that point it's a good idea to ask for the secretary's name. She may give you her first name or she may be more formal; whichever, it's essential that you make a note of her name in your business address book and use it whenever a female answers that phone.

The point of learning a secretary's name is that it helps to establish your relationship with her. Secretaries speak with lots of busy people all day long and they'll notice if someone takes the trouble to remember their name. It's a personal touch and it makes a difference.

If ever the secretary you've come to know is replaced, you'll start off at an advantage with her replacement. Suppose a client that you call regularly has a secretary named Susan. One day you call up, hear a woman's voice and say, "Hi, Susan. This is Jane Smith." If Susan has been replaced by a new secretary, the new woman is likely to say, "I'm sorry. Susan isn't here any longer. This is Arlene. Can I help you?" And that marks the beginning of a new relationship.

Since a secretary is the main barrier between you and your prospect it's always helpful to have her cooperation. If she can tell you the best time to reach her boss you'll save a lot of time and wasted effort by following her advice. If she says, "He'll be in Thursday but that's the day of the stockholders' meeting and he'll be preoccupied," then you know not to call on Thursday. If she says, "I'll tell you. Mr. Jones is always at his desk by eight o'clock every morning and no one ever calls until nine," then you know when to call if you want to be his first sales call of the day.

Before you ever call a prospect you should know exactly what you would say to a secretary's question, "What is the call in reference to?" And you should always know what you will say when you hear, "This is John Jones speaking." If you have only a minute or two on the telephone you don't want to have to ad lib. The goal of this initial telephone presentation is to make your prospect eager to *see you* . . . not to make him buy *your product*. The cardinal rule of appointment-getting is DON'T SELL IT ALL. If you attempt to give your whole presentation over the phone you'll do yourself a disservice on several counts.

First, by trying to cram all of your product information into a short phone call you'll suggest the possibility that a half-hour meeting is extraneous. Why should he bother to meet with you if you've already given your presentation?

Second, a reasonable presentation will probably keep you on the phone for about ten minutes, and ten minutes is a very long phone call in the middle of a business day. After the first few minutes your client will not be able to concentrate on what you're saying. He'll be too busy worrying about all the people he *wants* to talk to who can't get through his busy line.

Your job, when you get your prospect on the phone, is to convince him, in a very short time, that he should invest some *more* time to see you and what you're selling. Just as in the case of a sales presentation, you'll need to plan ahead of time just what you want to say and anticipate questions so that you don't get hit with anything uncomfortable. Don't plan on improvising!

When someone who works for Careers For Women gets a potential client she'll say something like this:

Hello. My name is Jane Jones. I represent a company called Careers For Women. We're a sales and marketing school for women and we're convinced that we have the best sales talent in the world going through our programs. We also have a hundred and twenty-five Fortune 500 clients who hire these saleswomen. Would it be possible for us to meet with you for fifteen minutes and explain in detail exactly what our service is?

Let's analyze the above approach. The first thing our saleswoman has done is introduce herself with her full name. Next, she's introduced the company. From that point she's gone into a very broad, nonspecific explanation of what our company does. And finally, she's dangled a piece of bait.

The bait consists of a claim and a substantiation of the claim. In the case of Careers For Women the prospect has to put together several pieces of information. First, he has to think about the fact that we call ourselves a school rather than an employment agency. Does that mean that he'll be hiring trained people? Second, he's being offered a source of sales-*women*. The government may be on his tail. Third, it's being suggested to him that many other companies are already in on the deal . . . except him. What has he got to lose? We're only asking for fifteen minutes.

The content of our initial telephone contact may vary somewhat. If a prospect has been recommended to us by a mutual friend, then we'll want to mention the friend's name. If a prospect asks, "Would you mind telling me some of the fabric manufacturers that you represent?" we have to be ready with a list of companies. The key factor when calling for an appointment, however, is to limit your information to an *enticement*.

If at First You Don't Succeed

There is, of course, always the possibility that you won't get an appointment on your first try. A client may say that your product doesn't interest him now and suggest that you try him again in a few months. He might even say flatly that he doesn't see any place for your product in his company.

If you believe that your product is appropriate to a company (even if *they* don't know it yet) it's your job to persevere. I once spoke with a man who said he had no free time in the next six months to see me. I asked about lunch. I asked about breakfast. I asked about cocktails. And he kept on saying how he'd be interested in hearing what I had to say but just didn't have time. Finally I said, "Look. I happen to know that your office is on the sixtieth floor of the World Trade Center. Since you seem to be interested in Careers For Women, and since the elevator ride must take a few minutes, how would it be if I met you on the ground floor tomorrow morning at nine o'clock and we rode up together?"

My suggestion may sound funny to you. Fortunately it sounded just as funny to the executive I was speaking with. I made him like me and like the idea of our meeting. Somehow he found a breakfast slot for me. As long as someone indicates that they *might* be interested in hearing you out, you have to persevere to get an appointment. Many business deals were started because an alert salesperson took a cab ride to the airport with a busy executive.

If someone says, "Call me in a month," you should make a note on your calendar for exactly one month from that date and make a point of getting back to him. You have to be consistent about calling clients if you want them to know that you're interested. Don't ever try to reach someone twice a week for a month, drop them for six months, and then begin with the two weekly phone calls again. That sort of erratic behavior indicates a lack of interest and seriousness.

Creativity, Thy Name Is Saleswoman

There are, of course, lots of ways to persevere when you want to get an appointment. Calling, calling and more calling can become a drag after a while and it may pay to apply a bit of creativity to your efforts. I honestly think that women have more of a flair for "creative selling" than men. Let me give you a few examples.

I have a friend who sells advertising space for a major national magazine. She spent a great deal of time pursuing a manufacturer of perfume and found that, despite her charm, she couldn't get past his secretary. After almost a month of trying, she met a friend who knew the man she was trying to contact and she grilled this woman to find out if there was any way at all that she could make her connection. She discovered that the perfume importer had a real "thing" for bubble gum. The next day she bought $60 worth of bubble gum and had it sent to his office. Do you have any idea how much bubble gum $60 will buy? Three days later she got an appointment.

One woman I placed with a textile company found it impossible to get in to see a dress manufacturer. She was convinced that her goods were particularly suited to the style of his line. She finally got him on the phone and he swore that he had no time at all to talk to her. "Listen," she said, "I know that you're busy and I don't want to waste your time, but you can't be too busy to have a cup of coffee and a bagel in the morning. If you meet with me for fifteen minutes I'll bring you a bagel with cream cheese and lox and a cup of coffee and you won't have to say a word. All you'll have to do is eat." He thought she was funny, he ate her bagel, and he bought her fabric!

Another woman I know was the sales manager for a fashion magazine. When she couldn't get in to see the single largest advertising director for cosmetics she sent him a director's chair with his name stenciled on the back of it. Along with the gift she enclosed a note that said, "To the man our sales staff most wants to meet with." He immediately picked up the phone and said, "Let's get together. I've got a chair open for you."

I once spent a good deal of time trying to reach Bonnie Wall, the assistant to the Director of Personnel at Hoffman LaRoche. LaRoche is one of the country's largest drug manufacturers and I was very interested in placing some women with them. I'd met Bonnie before and I knew that she was a real work-a-holic, but I also knew that she was a charming and sympathetic person. Finally, I sent her a dozen long-stemmed roses. The next day Bonnie Wall called me, laughing, and said, "I'm just calling to say I can't accept bribes but what can I do for you?"

The expenditure of a chair, bubble gum, bagels and lox, or roses doesn't mean a thing when you hold it against the money those women made from their clients. Usually if you pro-rate the cost of such things over a long period of time it adds up to pennies, but the people you treat with this sort of special attention never forget your effort.

The Saleswoman as Detective

You can also get appointments by discovering and solving a prospect's marketing problems. A saleswoman I placed several years ago wanted to get an appointment with the president of a watch company. She spent a reasonable time trying to get an appointment with him but had no success, so she went to several retail stores—Lord & Taylor, Saks Fifth Avenue, etc.—to find out how well his watches were selling.

She discovered that every time she asked the person behind the counter to show her one of her watches, she produced a watch that was clipped into a small display case. When she asked to try the watch on, the retail salesperson bent back the two little clips that held it to the case and handed it to her. When she returned the watch to the salesperson she noticed that rather than put it back into its individual case, she tossed it into a drawer behind the counter.

Apparently the two little clips that held the wristwatch in its display case couldn't be reused, and the manufacturer was having a devastatingly high number of broken watches returned from retail stores. The saleswoman wrote a letter to the president of the company saying who she was and why she wanted an appointment; but she added a note saying that she could solve the problem they were having with high returns of damaged merchandise.

The company's president called her as soon as he got her letter and asked her how she knew about their problem. Her explanation indicated that she was bright and clearly worth listening to.

The Appointment That Doesn't Happen

Even if you get through to a prospect and manage to set up an appointment, there are a number of things that could go wrong. And it's important that you respond to any such problem in a way that turns it to your advantage.

I am a firm believer in never confirming appointments. When you and your prospect agree to meet at two o'clock Thursday, that's it. At two you arrive. If you tell your prospect, "And I'll call in the morning just to confirm," you no longer have a *definite* appointment, you have a *tentative* one.

But what happens if your client is late or forgets the appointment entirely? It is your responsibility to protect your prospect's psychological position. Your client is not your husband, your son, your daughter, or your buddy. If any of those people are late you can do what you like. If your client is late it behooves you to be especially friendly and understanding.

The point of this "unnatural" behavior is that your prospect, when he's late, has put himself at a psychological disadvantage. He's inconvenienced you. You now are in a position to be emotionally generous; you can forgive. If you're nice and friendly he'll feel a bit like he owes you one, and that feeling can translate into a comfortable environment in which you can sell.

I once had an appointment with the Director of Personnel at a major pharmaceutical company. I waited over an hour, but he never showed.

After fifteen minutes his secretary began to get nervous and apologize. I told her not to worry.

After thirty minutes she began calling to locate him until I stopped her.

After forty-five minutes she said, "Mr. King, I can't imagine what has happened. He is never this late." Again I reassured her that I was very comfortable and getting a little work done. She directed me to the employees' cafeteria so that I could have a cup of coffee and I brought her back one, too.

When I finally had to leave after an hour, I was still cheerful and friendly to the secretary.

My prospect called me the next day, we rescheduled our appointment, and he became a client. As often happens, several months after he became a client he became a friend, and he later told me that there was no way he had even the slightest chance of not doing business with me after being more than an hour late for our first appointment. He said when he walked into his office his secretary stood up and demanded, "How could you do that to that nice Mr. King?"

CHAPTER

10

The Business Lunch

Many years ago I was invited to a function sponsored by Advertising Women of New York. The organization had set up a panel of media buyers, media planners, media supervisors and media directors to answer the question of some eighty-odd saleswomen. The intent of the symposium was to give the saleswomen an opportunity to get feedback on their various sales approaches and problems in an informal setting, free from the pressures of having to "make a sale." The idea appealed to me.

About two thirds of the way through the meeting a woman raised her hand and said, "How important is the business lunch?" I had no doubt what the answer to that question would be. I expected every panel member to say something like "Let me get something straight here. I'm hired by my clients to determine where the best places are to advertise their product. Whether or not you take me out and wine and dine me is inconsequential to that decision," or "Don't think that you're going to have any influence on my decision because you take me to a nice restaurant for lunch." Sounds good, doesn't it? That isn't, however, what I heard.

The first man to address the question said, "The business lunch is *very* important. This is a people business and you can't really learn anything about the person you're dealing with from a half-hour sales presentation three times a year. However, when you go out and have a lunch for an hour and a half you really get to know a person . . . to develop a sense of her character and whether or not you can trust her. I think that kind of encounter is very important."

The next panelist was quick to agree. "I think it's enormously important," he said, "but the reason I think it's so important is that it's fun! I enjoy going off and relaxing over a gracious lunch. That's the *enjoyment* side of business, and I firmly believe that business ought to have some enjoyment to it. Why should business associates only meet each other on a 'Here's what we're supposed to be talking about' basis?"

Every buyer on the panel that afternoon stressed the importance of the business lunch. Without exception they said that they looked forward to their lunches, that they welcomed them, and that they considered them crucial to successful business relationships. My prior notions about the importance of the business lunch were no longer important. What mattered was that all of the people women were selling to considered *lunching* important. Therefore LUNCHING WAS IMPORTANT!

As a result of the Advertising Women of New York's panel discussion I decided that it was very important for women to learn how to get the most from a business lunch. Many people—particularly women—always go to good restaurants as "passengers." Passengers simply don't notice the kinds of things that hosts need to be aware of. You don't notice the mechanics of tipping. You don't know how you happen to end up sitting in one area of the restaurant instead of another. You *might* notice your host say something to the headwaiter, but you don't know what it is that's being said and how all of the arrangements of your lunch came to pass. You need to know something about ordering an appropriate wine. Essentially, you must learn to be as poised in the driver's seat as you are when you're a passenger. It's very important, in terms of the role you take in the business world, that you learn how to host a lunch. If you defer the host's privileges (which begin with suggesting a restaurant and making a reservation) to the person you're entertaining just because he's a man, you'll dilute your own responsibility.

About five months after the panel discussion I got a call from a saleswoman I had placed with a publication. "David," she said, "do me a favor. Let me buy you breakfast and discuss some problems I've been having." Over our coffee and eggs she discussed a long list of problems involving straightening out her account list, using the telephone, cleaning up the mess of her predecessor—all things I considered eminently "fixable." There was clearly no problem in dealing with what *she* considered to be her problems. But within a few minutes after this woman began to butter her toast it was evident that she had another big problem—one she knew nothing about. That woman, at breakfast, displayed the worst table manners I have ever seen, and she was in an industry that required a great deal of "meal entertaining." As a result of our breakfast I became very specific and very frank in a discussion of her eating etiquette, but I'd suggest that you examine yourself in terms of what I'm saying. By the time we're adults the way we eat has become almost a reflex. We all have idiosyncrasies. If you're about to do a great deal of business entertaining you're going to have to really think about how you eat. It may be that nothing I saw applies to you, but since I eat nearly every meal with some business associate I have a great opportunity to observe people eating, and I'm very familiar with "quirks." You may be the *least* informed about your table manners. When's the last time you watched yourself eat with any sort of critical eye?

Two Kinds of Lunches

In my mind there are basically two kinds of client lunches: the normal business lunch and the celebration. The first takes place because you have something to discuss but you couldn't get on the client's schedule. Such a lunch shouldn't be set up unless you already know and have met with the client. With rare exceptions, it's inappropriate to set up a lunch with a total stranger. If you've already had dealings with a man or woman, and you've made every effort to get on his or her schedule without success, it's entirely proper to say, "Do you have any breakfasts or lunches free?" (You can always substitute breakfast for lunch in this circumstance.)

Such an invitation *may* get you an appointment. And that's precisely what you'll have—an *appointment*. Keep in mind that these appointments are not celebrations. You're meeting with a very busy person, and the purpose of your meeting is to discuss business.

The most important thing for you to do at such lunches is to set things up so that you'll have every opportunity to get your information across. Since your goal is to make a sales presentation within the forty-five minutes or so that you're together it's likely that you'll need to do a lot of talking; which means that you can't be overly occupied with the tasks of eating. If you order something that's hot and whole (like a steak or a piece of fish) your client will probably be paying more attention to the progress of your "eating" than to what you're saying. He may interrupt you occasionally to ask, "Why don't you eat?" or "Look at your food, it's going to get cold." In such instances the nature of the food on your plate will call attention to the fact that you're selling, and as I've said, the best kind of selling doesn't feel like SELLING.

You can best handle that kind of situation by ordering something that you can take a few forkfuls of and then push around on your plate. When you're eating lobster salad your client won't have to think about whether or not your food is getting cold. You'll be able to hold a fork in your hand rather than juggle with a knife, and the "eating process" will recede into the background.

You have to judge just how much time you'll need to convey all the information crucial to your sales presentation. If you need the entire lunch, then begin your presentation at the beginning and end it over coffee. If you think that your presentation will only take as long as dessert, then use the beginning of the lunch to establish yourself: your interests; the pleasure you take in your work; the things that you might have in common with the person sitting across from you. But you must be certain when you have this kind of a business lunch that you never get so absorbed with your food that you forget what you're there for.

The second kind of business lunch is probably more important and certainly more fun. This is the sumptuous and leisurely lunch: the celebration. You are taking a client out and you want him to know that he's going to have a special treat. Your choice of restaurant, the amount of money that you spend and the easy, relaxed way in which you spend it, all tell your client that you want to do something nice for him. Your goal is to establish rapport and to create a very subtle sense of psychological indebtedness. You might call up your client and say something like, "Listen, I think it's time that my company took *us* out for a lavish, leisurely lunch. Let's go to some spectacular restaurant and blow 'em away." And make sure that you set aside two hours for yourself because you won't get back before then.

Remember the men at the panel discussion who felt that the business lunch was important? They liked the idea of having fun. They'll have no difficulty setting aside the two hours for a "big" lunch, and they'll remember it the next time you call.

Breakfast, Lunch, Cocktails and Dinner

Every meal can be used for business entertaining. It used to be that lunch was *the* time, but all of that has changed. Very busy, important executives have become fond of making "breakfast dates." The implication of a breakfast date is that you're so enormously busy and that your schedule is so tightly packed that you have to resort to an early morning meeting.

One woman I placed in advertising space sales told me that she actually preferred breakfast dates because they usually didn't require any drinking. She had a real problem combining alcohol and business and the breakfast date was a graceful solution for her. (I'll discuss the matter of drinking in more detail later.)

Cocktails are also a popular setting for a business meeting. If you hate drinking or a drinking milieu, they may not be the best solution for you. But even if you order a non-alcoholic beverage there's a very relaxed atmosphere over cocktails and you may find it a comfortable way to get to know a client or prospect.

Throughout this chapter I'll concentrate on the business *lunch*. Any of the information I give you can be generalized to every other eating–entertaining situation. Since lunch usually includes cocktails and the meal involves anything that might arise in a breakfast or dinner situation, it's a good place to generalize from. And lunch is still the most popular time for business entertaining.

Making the Lunch Date

The Restaurant

You're ready to ask a client to lunch. What do you do? First of all, before you even pick up the phone, it's a good idea to check with other people on your sales force or in your company to find out which restaurants they recommend. In some big cities restaurants are actually specific to industries. New York has some restaurants that are always filled with people in publishing, and others that are favorite haunts for Madison Avenue advertising executives. People in the garment district often eat in the same place.

I can't run down a list of every restaurant in the country and tell you where to eat, but a little bit of research before you make your phone call will do the job. The most important thing is for you to approach your prospect with information: "Hi, John. I think it would be nice if we got together for lunch? How about The Palm?" Don't rely on your prospect to recommend a restaurant. He'll take you to *his* favorite place where the captain knows *him,* and where *he* will be treated as host.

It's also a good idea for you to be prepared with the names of a few restaurants when you call your prospect. You might suggest an Italian place and discover that he's allergic to tomatoes. It's your responsibility to be prepared with an alternative . . . and an alternative . . . and an alternative.

The Phone Call

It's time to make the call. Once you get involved in sales you'll discover how important a calendar is. Never make a lunch date unless you have your calendar sitting in front of you. Everyone in business has meetings, appointments, lunches, dinners, cocktail dates, and so on. You should never assume that you can call someone up and make a lunch date for that day. Some people are actually booked for a month in advance. The best thing for you to do is explain that you'd like to make a date and say, "When's the best time for you?"

Your client may say, "I've got a cancellation on Friday," or, "Look, I'm not free for a couple of weeks, but let's write it down so we know we've got a date." If your calendar is very booked you should make that clear from the beginning of your conversation. You might say, "I'm free starting next week. When's best for you?" You don't ever want to be in a situation where your client suggests date after date and you say, "No, I'm busy, no, I'm busy." After a few of those he'll begin to wonder why you brought the subject of a lunch up in the first place.

Once you've agreed on a date and time it's up to you to suggest a restaurant. If you've done your preparation you shouldn't have a problem. In most cases a client won't take issue with the restaurant you suggest.

Pre-Meal Planning

When you go to a good restaurant there's a certain amount of pre-planning that you should do. You can take care of these arrangements on the phone, or you can make a point of arriving early, before your client.

Credit Cards

The first thing you have to find out about are the kinds of credit cards that the restaurant accepts. Never assume that a restaurant will accept every card. You may be embarrassed at the end of your meal.

Preferred Seating

Next, find out about *preferred seating*. If you haven't made the restaurant route before, you won't have any problem finding out what the good restaurants are. You can simply ask friends or people in your business, "What's a good restaurant in such and such area?" and they'll tell you. But many of the better restaurants have preferred seating. If your client is sophisticated and aware of the seating arrangement in a particular restaurant he may be very peeved to find himself in the "wrong place." It's your responsibility as host to see to such matters.

Let me give you a few examples of "preferred seating" in New York. At the Four Seasons preferred seating is in the Poolroom, not the room with the bar. At "21," a very posh restaurant, preferred seating is downstairs. Upstairs at Orsini's there is an aisle that ends in a cul-de-sac. The only people that sit on the aisle are out-of-towners who don't know any better. People in the know are aware that the cul-de-sac is the preferred place to be seated. If you're looking for a rule of thumb about where "preferred seating" is, you can stop looking. Some preferred seating is dictated by the view or by a specific room. In other cases it's just a matter of tradition. The only way to find out where the preferred seating is, is to ask.

This may all sound like nonsense to you, but I can assure you that many of the people you'll be dealing with won't take it as lightly. If you arrive early and are seated on the aisle in Orsini's, your client may actually be embarrassed to be seen there. You need never be ashamed to inquire about preferred seating.

If, when you call to make your reservation, you say, "My name is Jane Jones. This restaurant was very highly recommended to me but I've never eaten here. Is there preferred seating?" the person taking your reservation will always fill you in. They may say, "Many of our customers prefer to sit in the front room, but our other rooms are equally nice." That's your cue. Make it clear where you want to sit, and make certain to ask the name of the person with whom you're speaking. Asking a name means that any problems will be traceable, and it also implies that you might leave a tip—which you're not obliged to do.

Dress

Another aspect of pre-meal planning involves checking the dress requirements. Although such requirements are becoming less important, and virtually every client you entertain will be in either a suit or a sports coat, there are still some restaurants where a man in a turtleneck can't get in. At "21" you cannot get in without a tie and jacket; and they take great pride in turning away important people who do not have on ties and jackets. There are still a couple of restaurants where women wearing slacks—however fine the slacks suit may be—will not be admitted. It's always best to check for such things before they become a problem.

Kind of Seating

You should also make a point of asking about the *kinds* of tables in a given restaurant. You will always be more comfortable with *across-seating,* rather than *adjacent* (or *banquette*) seating. It's awkward and unnatural to have someone sitting next to you on a business lunch. Every time you want to talk you'll have to turn your head, and you lose all eye contact while you're eating. There's also something uncomfortably intimate about adjacent seating.

There will be times when you'll have difficulty getting across-seating. The Coach House—which is easily the best restaurant in Greenwich Village—does not have across-seating for two.

Kind of Menu

You also must take care to be sensitive to the kind of menu that you're going to run into. It's bad form, even if you speak fluent French, to take someone to a French restaurant if he won't understand a thing on the menu. You might inquire, when you make your lunch date, if your client likes French food. If he says it's a favorite, then you can assume that he'll be reasonably familiar with a French menu. If he says he doesn't like it, then move on to another cuisine. There are many restaurants in big cities where the entire menu is written in French, and it's a horror story for two people to rely on a captain to translate an entire menu. You can't go down the sheet saying, "What's this? And what's this? And what's this?" If you ask that question more than once at a place like Lutèce in New York, you'll find that you're talking to yourself. The captain will have left your table to request a change of stations before you get to your third question.

The important thing is for you to be prepared to host a lunch with a certain amount of grace. And to do that you have to be aware of the customs, whether you like them or not.

Picking Up the Tab

If you suspect that your client will be uncomfortable when you pick up the check, you may want to consider prepaying the lunch. Arrive ahead of time and inform the captain that *you* are the one who's entertaining. In order to avoid a problem you can give him your credit card and let him run it through his machine. Before the meal you can sign it and state what percentage of tip you want for the captain and for the waiter. If you ask them they will mail you your receipt, and the bill for your meal need never come to the table.

A somewhat less drastic way of avoiding problems would be simply to remind the captain ahead of time that you're the host. At the end of the meal he'll make a point of presenting you—not your guest—with the check. If you don't make the point, waiters and captain may still automatically give the check to the man at the table. It's an old habit and it takes time to break.

If there's one restaurant that you do most of your entertaining in, it may be possible for you to open a restaurant account. At the end of your meal you simply sign your check and wait for a bill at the end of the month.

Restrooms

It's always a good idea for you to find out ahead of time where the restrooms are. The fact that you know where they are will, first of all, establish that you are familiar with the restaurant. It will also save your client the time and the hassle of wandering around asking people.

Tablecloths and Napkins

You might want to check out what kinds of tablecloths and napkins they have in a restaurant you're planning to visit. There are certain restaurants that are notorious for tablecloths that leave you covered with lint. You'll want to avoid them. It's terribly unpleasant to spend your afternoon picking lint and threads off your clothing.

Finally, you mustn't feel inhibited about asking any of these questions. If you like a restaurant and want to go there regularly, you'll find that the more things you do to insure that you're going to have control of the meal, the more likely everyone in that restaurant is to remember and respect you. Obviously, you'll want to deal with things in a quiet, genteel way, but it's entirely possible, if you've made the right impression, to have a maître d', a captain, and a waiter greet you personally by your second visit. If they feel that they're appreciated—that their efforts to please you have been noticed—they'll knock themselves out to make you happy.

Remember that a captain loves the idea that there's one more person out there who's going to request him by name, because everyone associated with the restaurant will get the impression that he's doing a good job. They *want* you to let them know what you want.

The Meal

Pacing the Business

When do you talk business? When do you eat? How do you manage to do both at the same time? Learning to pace a business lunch usually requires some time and experience. The most important thing for you to keep in mind is that your cues should come from the person you're entertaining. One way or another you're going to have to find out from that person if he's interested in talking about his personal life or his business life and precisely when he's ready to start talking about each one.

If you're entertaining a client who seems interested in discussing his crabgrass or the last movie he saw, you have to be very careful about introducing business. The last thing in the world that you want to sound like is a *sales*man. If your prospect is talking about a movie and you say, "Did I mention that my new product can do X, Y, and Z simultaneously?" you're going to trigger an alarm in your prospect's head. The alarm, which I've mentioned before and will continue to mention, will say, "Watch out for this lady. She's trying to sell, and she's gonna pull a fast one if I'm not on my guard."

The best way to "read" your client is to get him talking. You may discover that when you say, "I'm so pleased that we're finally getting to meet and spend some time with each other," your client will respond with, "I am also. How long have you been in sales? It's so nice to see more women in the field."

That kind of response says, "Let's get to know each other," and you can begin to talk about yourself and listen to him talk about himself. If the client responds to your initial statement by saying, "I'm glad we have a chance to get together as well. I've had trouble understanding the functioning of X, Y, and Z in my particular kind of business," then you know that it's time to dive right in.

By the time you're ready to order you should have a sense of your prospect's personality. Keep putting out feelers, and take care in how you read his responses. And always let your client direct the conversation so that *he'll* feel comfortable. If you don't get a chance to discuss your product in detail, use a follow-up letter or make an appointment to see the client in his office.

Most frequently business is discussed over drinks and over coffee and dessert. Somehow people have an easier time talking and concentrating when they're coping with a liquid than they do when they have to cut and chew. The point of meal-entertaining is to sell, and it's up to you to create an environment that will make your prospect feel like buying.

Cocktails

Most business lunches begin with cocktails. Ideally, cocktails should be a relaxed, leisurely time for you to get acquainted (reacquainted), and it should set the pace and tone of your relationship. It should, above all, be friendly. There are several things to be considered if the cocktail time is to be successful.

First, always keep in mind that *you* are the one who controls the amount of alcohol that you drink. In order for a drink to get into your mouth you have to pick up the glass, bring it to your lips, sip, and swallow. Once you understand the degree to which you're in control, there should be no anxiety about drinking too much. You need only take fewer or smaller sips if you want to drink less. You can always alternate between your cocktail glass and your water glass. However you handle the situation, it's still you who is in control.

If you don't like alcohol, don't trust yourself with alcohol, are allergic to alcohol, or for any other reason want to avoid it, you have several options. Consider your client's attitude toward cocktails. If he's relaxed and not a particularly big drinker, you can probably order something that's not alcoholic.

But there are people who find it uncomfortable to drink when they're sitting across from someone who isn't keeping pace. I once heard someone describe his lunch date this way: "She's a real drag. She doesn't drink." If you're going to have lunch with someone who equates not drinking with being a drag you can arrange with the captain ahead of time to keep the alcohol out of your drink—regardless of what you order. He'll understand precisely what you want if you say, "Look, when I ask for a gin and tonic, please leave out the gin," or "When I order a Bloody Mary, don't put any vodka in it." They run across this sort of thing every day.

Service

The cocktail period should, as I said, be leisurely. There's no need for you to feel rushed about ordering. It's easy to be intimidated by a very posh restaurant. You may be talking for a while over drinks and the captain may come up and ask if you're ready to order. It's important for you to understand that he doesn't mean, "You had better order now or we're going to throw you out." He means precisely what he says. He's asking a question, and if you aren't ready yet there's nothing wrong with saying, "We're not quite ready. Give us a few minutes," or "Not just yet, thanks. I'll let you know when we're ready to order."

If the service is crisper than you want, it can interfere

with a leisurely meal. A busboy or a waiter may clean the table prematurely. They might clear away your plate while your client is still eating. This kind of service may make your client feel pressured to eat quickly and it's up to you to correct the problem. You need only tell the captain that you're entertaining someone who's important to you and you don't want the meal to be rushed. He'll make an effort to hold back the waiter. He'll see to it that they don't clear any of the dishes for a given course until both parties are finished eating. Remember what I said earlier about asserting control over your meal. No one will take offense at your efforts to have things done nicely.

The most important thing to remember about eating in a fine restaurant (or any restaurant for that matter) is that you must *always avoid scenes*. Whatever the reason for a scene may be, you'll only end up embarrassing yourself and your client. If you have a stain on your water glass the likelihood is that the glasses were sterilized in hot water and the "lipstick" just didn't come off. Call over the captain. (You don't have to actually call. He will be standing somewhere in the room surveying his tables, waiting for someone to catch his eye.) Simply say, "Do me a favor. Will you get me another glass." He'll know what that means. He isn't going to cause any problem over it.

The same goes for a utensil. If you notice some egg yolk on your fork, don't call the waiter over and say, "Look at this. This is disgusting. There's dirt on my fork." Just ask for another one. They'll know something is wrong and take care of it discreetly. Your goal is to have a nice lunch—not to chastise or to win a point. If your food isn't prepared as you ordered it, they'll take it back without a fuss. There is virtually never a reason to cause a scene.

It's usually a good idea to lodge any complaints away from the table. If the service is too fast or too slow, excuse yourself for a moment. On your way to the ladies' room you can stop and talk with the captain. Always try to be discreet. Don't adopt an imperious tone when you talk to the people who are serving you. You'll get a lot more accomplished if you're friendly. You shouldn't push, and you shouldn't let yourself be pushed around.

Ordering

Most women know the nonperson feeling of sitting at a table and having a captain ask the man (who might even be their guest), "And what will the young lady be having?" That kind of communication is a throwback to childhood. Do you remember shopping for clothing with your mother and listening to the "salesgirl" ask, "Does she like blue dresses?" and your mother saying, "Yes, but she'd prefer something in white for now."

When you're hosting a lunch it must be perfectly clear to everyone that *you* are the host. The best way to assert this to the captain (or whoever takes your order) is to begin talking. It's your job to ask for the menus. When he approaches your table with pencil in hand you might ask, "What would you suggest today?" That sort of question will cue him to direct his talk to you.

When it actually comes to ordering you have a choice. If you're comfortable doing all of the ordering it's entirely proper for you to ask your guest what he'll be having, and for *you* to give the order to the captain for both of you. That kind of behavior can set the tone for successful business entertaining. Ideally, your guest should get the feeling that he's being taken care of.

If you think your guest would arch his back at the idea of a woman "speaking for him," then you can retain your host-power in another way. When the captain comes to take an order you can say to your guest—in the presence of the captain—"Are you ready to order yet?" Then let him order for himself. Even though you aren't doing all of the ordering, your question will make it clear to everyone that you're acknowledging your responsibilities as host.

Always make an effort to keep track of what you've ordered and how much the bill will come to. You need only have a rough idea—round things off to zero—but it's always good to have some idea where you stand before the check arrives. Since you may be entertaining a male client who is unaccustomed to being taken out by a woman, you'll want to do everything in your power to make him feel comfortable with the new situation—short of relinquishing your role as host. It's likely that he'll feel particularly uncomfortable with the idea of your paying for the lunch. If you haven't opted to prepay the check, you'll still want to take as little time with the paying process as possible. If you hold the check up to the light and start adding the columns, you may cause your guest some embarrassment. If you have a rough idea of what the total should be—within five dollars—then you can take care of business quickly.

Your Captain

It is the captain's service—not the waiter's—that determines how well your meal goes. He'll prepare any parts of the meal that should be prepared at tableside. He'll control the pacing of the meal. If there's any favor that you want, he'll be the one to take care of you. The waiter is actually an assistant to the captain the way the busboy is an assistant to the waiter. It will be worth your while to establish a relationship with a particularly good captain, especially if you want to frequent his restaurant.

How do you go about establishing this relationship? First, make a point of asking his name, and request one of his tables when you make your reservation. By doing this you're letting his boss know that he's doing a good job, and he'll appreciate your attention.

Second, always watch him when he prepares something tableside. The reason certain dishes are prepared at your table rather than in the kitchen is that they involve something of a ceremony. Their preparation is supposed to be an attractive part of your meal—a tableside show. It's rude to ignore this demonstration. You should stop talking, turn your head, watch what's being done and even make a brief comment to show your appreciation—"Lovely" will do just fine. Captains, like all of us, like to know that they're being appreciated, and it takes very little effort on your part to tend to their needs.

Finally, if you have a good captain, stick with him. Don't keep playing Russian roulette with captains. It may happen that your captain is moved to a less desirable station. When that happens you have to decide which is more important—preferred seating or your captain. There are ways to handle either decision with some delicacy. You can always explain to your client that this isn't the best place to sit, but you have a particular allegiance to this captain. Your client will understand, and may even be impressed that you have a personal relationship with the people serving you. They know you.

You can also sit elsewhere while your captain has the less desirable assignment if you make a point of explaining to your captain that your client is kind of a snob and he always wants to sit in the preferred area. Your captain will be sympathetic to your situation.

Tipping

Proper tipping is very important. It is, obviously, a good, tangible way to show your appreciation. There are several rules about tipping which dictate when to tip and how much to tip, and it's important for you to be familiar with the whole procedure.

First, don't tip until the end of your meal. An exception might be if you're in a restaurant and told that there are no tables available. Since you'll always make a reservation, such a circumstance is most unusual, but if you should "fall into" a place you'll probably pick up a signal that says you can *buy* a table even though there "are no tables available." Be discreet and sound like you're hip—like you know what's happening. You might say to the maître d', "Is there no way that I can get it?" or "Is there no amount of money in the world that can get me into there?" If you get a positive signal, fold a five dollar bill into your palm and shake the man's hand. It's incredible what five dollars will do for you. But don't start waving your money in the air. It's not a flag.

If you offer the money and they don't accept, you'll end up feeling very awkward, so it's a bit of a touch-and-go situation.

Normal tipping—the tipping that takes place after you've completed your meal is 15 percent for the waiter and 10 percent for the captain. Never assume that the restaurant will automatically divide your tip between the captain and the waiter. If you just leave a 25 percent tip without indicating 10 percent for the captain, the entire amount will go to the waiter.

When you get your credit card slip there will probably be a line for you to note the tip. If there are two lines then you can write in "waiter" and "captain" and indicate the proper amount next to each title. If there is only one line, then it's up to you to draw a second, on which you should note your captain's tip. Tipping is *your* responsibility.

There may be circumstances in which you'll want to tip something extra. If your company has limited you to 25 percent for gratuities, you'll have to cut back on one person's tip to reward another. Under no circumstances should you cut back on the captain's tip—unless you never want to see him again. You can cut back on the waiter's tip, but it should never be reduced to less than 12½ percent. Less than that is dangerous—he'll begin to make sounds.

Good tipping for a great captain means $5 or 15 percent. If he's done things to make the meal very special he deserves a special tip, and moving from the usual 10 percent up to 15 percent is appropriate.

The wine steward is usually a man who wears a silver chain around his neck and comes over to deliver, or discuss, the wine list. He is only deserving of a tip if he does two things. First, he must put you on to an especially good wine in your price range. And second, he must be between you and the door after you've paid for your meal. Never take care of the wine steward's tip at the table. If, in fact, he is standing between you and the door, you should put $2 in your palm and shake his hand. They are remarkably good at getting those two bills out of your hand in a delicate fashion. Don't worry about it being awkward.

The maître d' should be tipped only if he does something very special for you. But if you go to a restaurant frequently (once a week is considered frequent) it's a good idea to give the maître d' $5 every six weeks or so and say, "Thanks for taking care of me when I'm here." That sort of tip is more than adequate and will insure you a great welcome whenever you come to eat.

Paying by Cash

Always try to pay for your lunch with a credit card. It's awkward to get involved with cash when you begin having $50 lunches. If you absolutely must pay for your lunch by cash, you can leave the waiter's tip on the table. The captain's tip should be handed to him. Don't leave it on the table lest it be confused with the waiter's tip.

Wine

There's not a great deal you need to know about wine in order to entertain a client. Yet wine lists can be intimidating, and there are all sorts of myths about wine that seem designed to make you feel inadequate. The most important thing for you to remember is that no one expects you to be an expert. Not many people are wine experts, and it's certainly not a requirement for a good saleswoman. The point of all this reassurance is that you should never try to make it look like you know a lot about wines unless you actually do. Don't spend fifteen minutes discussing "bouquet" and how you like to "let it breathe." Unless you use those expressions all the time in your daily life—which few of us do—they're going to sound pretentious and phony.

Always keep in mind that if you're lunching with a client who—unknown to you—knows a great deal about wine, he'll see through an act in a matter of minutes. And if he thinks you're a phony when it comes to wine, he won't have much of a basis for trusting you when it comes to other things.

What to Order

Let's start with basics. Wine comes in a variety of three colors: red, white, or pink, and the pink wines are called rosés. The one thing you should know about rosés is that they are not a combination of red and white wines. There used to be rules about what color wine one should order depending on what you were eating. The old rules aren't as strictly adhered to today as they once were, but it's probably a good idea for you to know what they were.

Essentially, heavier (or heartier) wines were had with heavier meals. If you ordered a steak, or a stew, then you would order a red wine with a fairly strong flavor. Ideally, the food wouldn't overpower the wine and vice versa.

If you ordered fish, or fowl, it was considered more appropriate to order a lighter tasting wine—which usually meant a white wine. Once again, the rationale was that a delicate wine was more suited to a delicate meal.

The old rules were quite elaborate. It was said that rosé and champagne would go with any dish, but champagne was generally mated with very delicate or sweet food. Rosé has, traditionally, been looked down upon by wine connoisseurs as generally lacking in flavor. There were special wines—usually very sweet ones—that were to be had after a meal, on their own. They were considered a sophisticated alternative to dessert.

The thrust of all of the old rules was "compatibility." Nowadays, people order pretty much whatever they want, however they want it. At one time a wine steward might have fainted at the suggestion of chilling a burgundy—a hearty red wine. Today, if you prefer your red wines chilled, then you can have them chilled.

If you are ordering a red wine, always order a Beaujolais (pronounced bō-ja-lā). It is a light red wine that reaches its peak early. I'll explain.

All wines have what is called a peak—a certain time when they are at their best. Burgundy and Bordeaux wines don't reach their peak until they're ten to fifteen years old. Since restaurants have to buy them and wait years before they serve them (almost like an investment), a good Bordeaux or mature Burgundy, at its peak, will be very expensive. If you drink it before its peak it will still be expensive, but it won't be particularly good.

Since Beaujolais is meant to be drunk early, it doesn't require any aging. A Beaujolais at $7 a bottle is *always* better than a premature Burgundy or a Bordeaux. Isn't that even easier than the chart?

White wines, like Beaujolais, should be had young. In general, don't drink white wines that are over three years old. They have short lives, and after they've reached their peak they plummet quickly.

The List

You always order wine from a wine list. In fact, if both you and your client are ordering wine as a cocktail, rather than ask for a glass of the house wine you should ask to see the list and order a half-bottle of something light.

Wine lists look different in different restaurants. Some may be simple lists divided by color. In some instances a wine list will look like an album of labels. Whichever, there are several things to look for. You want to know the name, the year, the kind of wine (Beaujolais, Burgundy, Bordeaux, etc.) and the bin number. The bin number will help you in ordering if you have trouble with pronunciation. Some of the long French or German names can be quite a mouthful.

Tasting

After you have selected a wine, the wine steward (or the captain) will bring you the bottle and hold it in front of you for a moment. Your job, at that point, is to read the label and be certain that it's what you ordered. If it is, you'll nod, say, "Fine," or in some way convey your approval. The moment you do that, the wine becomes yours and the bottle will be opened. If, at any point after you nodded your approval, you discover that the wine isn't what you ordered, it's too late to do anything about it.

If the steward places the cork on the table after he's opened the bottle you can simply touch it or turn it over. DO

NOT SMELL THE CORK! Smelling the cork is a sure way to indicate that you don't know what you're doing. There's nothing to be told by the way a cork smells. The stain on the cork merely indicates whether or not the wine has been stored correctly—with the liquid slanting down toward the neck of the bottle—and no air was able to seep into the bottle. If the steward doesn't put the cork on the table, you needn't bother to ask him for it. It just isn't very important.

Once you get past the cork the steward will pour a little bit of wine into your glass. Don't make a production number out of this part of the wine ceremony. Don't spin the liquid vigorously in the glass. Don't hold it up to the light. Don't stick your nose into the glass and inhale. Don't pull a thermometer out of your bag and take the wine's temperature. All you need to do is swish the glass slightly—and I mean a simple turn of the wrist—and taste it.

The only time you should send a bottle of wine back is if it tastes like vinegar. When wine goes bad it tastes just like vinegar. Beyond that extreme, you should say, "Thank you, it's fine," and go about your meal. Don't ever look at a wine steward and say, "I don't think it's quite right," or "I just don't know." If it's not clearly, unquestionably, awfully bad, then it's drinkable . . . and you should be drinking it.

Service

Wine glasses should never be more than half filled. If you have an overzealous waiter or captain who's filling your glasses too high, you're certainly within your rights to correct the situation. As always, you want to be tactful. "Please don't put that much in the glasses" will do fine. It's always better to correct service off-stage.

At this point you've got all the information you'll need to move from the passenger seat over into the driver's seat with regard to lunching. The point of all the information in this chapter is not to intimidate you. If you do something wrong, bells and sirens won't begin to ring. But hopefully, all of this information will make it easier for you to relax. If you've read the chapter carefully, nothing will come up that you aren't prepared to handle. Enjoy!

11

How to Organize Yourself and Manage Your Time

You know by now that there are certain ratios you need to be aware of in sales. If you make three sales a week, but have to make fifteen calls to get those sales, your sales-to-calls ratio is 3:15. Most sales instruction is concerned with increasing the top number of your ratio—your number of sales. How do you turn 3:15 into 5:15? The emphasis in that approach is usually placed on improving your sales presentation.

But there are other approaches you can take to improve your sales-to-calls ratio. It may be that you're already giving a spectacular sales presentation. It may be that 3:15 is the best ratio you can get. If that's the case the only way for you to increase your total number of sales will be to pay attention to the bottom number of the ratio—your number of calls per week. That bottom figure doesn't have anything to do with actual sales talent, yet it's vital to your sales success. The key to improving the bottom half of your sales-to-calls ratio lies in learning how to best allocate your energies and your time.

I worked for someone in 1967 whom I still consider to

be the only true business genius I've ever known. He was eccentric, he was a screamer, and everyone who worked for him found him terrifying; but there was no getting around the fact that the man was a genius when it came to business. This man kept a little plaque on his desk that said:

EVERYONE HAS AN EQUAL AMOUNT OF TIME GIVEN HIM EACH DAY, AND ONCE THIS IS EXPENDED, IT CANNOT BE REPLACED AT ANY PRICE. AS A MATTER OF FACT, YOUR TIME IS YOUR LIFE: WHEN YOU WASTE TIME, YOU WASTE YOUR LIFE.

How do you find the time to make more sales calls? First of all you've got to get yourself organized.

Time to Organize

Friends

Most people who know me in a peripheral way think that I'm a gregarious person. I'm not. Actually I'm something of an introvert. I never have more than a few good friends, and —outside of a strictly business context—I don't spend a lot of time talking to people I don't know well.

At some point I realized that I spent an enormous amount of time with people who weren't important to me. I probably spent time with them because I once had time to spare. As I got more involved in my work, and as I learned to value my time for what it was worth, I recognized that I had to do something about all those evenings that "didn't matter." The first thing I did was eliminate "time-wasting" people. That may sound a bit harsh to you, but consider for a few minutes who your friends really are.

In fact, make a list of your "friends." You'll discover that you've collected a lot of people who are no longer particularly interesting to you but whom you feel obliged to see from time to time. Those people are taking your time, and according to my ex-boss, they are taking your life.

Once you've evaluated the bottom half of your "friend" list, start training everyone to respect the fact that you're a career woman.

Be Firm

You really have to learn to be decisive when you talk to people. You'll save yourself a lot of time when you learn to say "no." Try to put yourself in the following situation. A "friend" from the bottom half of your list calls and says she has two tickets to a show/the circus/the ballet/a movie for the following Thursday night. You have an important meeting first thing Friday morning and know that come Thursday evening you should be reading your notes on the clients you'll be seeing and reading some new literature on your product.

Normally you'd say, "Gee. I don't know. It sounds interesting. Let me see if I can work it out and I'll get back to you." That response means that you're going to waste time to call back and say you have a conflict. And that time will be lost from your work. And that lost time might, at some point, have been spent with someone from the top of your list!

You've learned to give a qualified answer because somehow it seems more polite than being decisive and negative. In fact, the issue here has nothing to do with "politeness." You can learn to say, in a very polite voice, "I'm sorry but it's absolutely impossible for me to do anything this month. But thanks for thinking of me," or "I'm so tightly squeezed for time that I can barely write a letter. After things calm down and my schedule lightens up I'll give you a call."

It's easy to learn to respond that way and it puts the ball

in your corner. If you should decide, in a month, that you miss the friend you can always give him/her a call and readjust your list.

Plan Ahead

There are several areas in which you can plan ahead. I always suggest that you keep your schedule very tight for two weeks into the future. Don't let yourself look like someone who has time on her hands. If you look like you have a lot of time you'll find lots of people who are willing to waste it for you.

People will begin to treat you accordingly. Stay in motion. Don't talk or move at too leisurely a pace. If someone drops by to see you for a minute, look at your watch and remain standing. Do you project the impression that you're busy?

You can also plan ahead when you arrange a meeting. Pre-planning for a meeting means a prepared agenda. If everyone gets a written agenda for any meeting you call they'll anticipate a meeting with structure—not just a meeting to kick ideas around. Ideally, an agenda will give them the chance to prepare themselves ahead of time. Most people aren't concise when they talk off the cuff, and you don't need to waste time waiting for everyone to warm up and get to the point.

If you run your meetings by agenda you'll develop a healthy skepticism for people who are overly fond of "brainstorming." All too often brainstorming sessions turn into free-for-all bull sessions. Executives can spend entire mornings and afternoons in meetings where nothing gets said. You could be using that time to increase the bottom figure in your ratio.

I've also found pre-planning helpful outside of the office. I never go to the bank on a Friday afternoon at one o'clock. My experience has indicated that, without exception, the bank will be crowded at lunchtime just before a weekend. I also buy subway tokens ahead of time whenever I happen to be around a token booth that has no line. When I'm working from our L.A. office I use a car. I never wait until my tank is empty (and I'm rushing to a meeting) before I get it filled.

This sort of pre-planning isn't at all foreign to women. If, until now, it's been your job to keep a cupboard well stocked, then you're in the habit of buying six cans of tuna fish when you notice you've only got two cans left on your shelf.

It's usually pretty easy to avoid waiting on lines. Doing things at the last possible moment is guaranteed to cost you time. If you're alert you'll take notice of where and when you run into crowds and avoid making the same mistake twice.

How to Read a Letter

Remember that eccentric genius I worked for in 1967? The one with the plaque on his desk? He actually taught me how to read a letter. When you get behind in your work—and most of us do—you'll usually find a stack of papers in one corner of your desk. The stack is composed of all the letters that you read but were too busy to deal with at the time.

Usually, when the stack gets high enough you decide that you've got to catch up. And you start at the top and reread each letter so that you can take care of it. My main rule about letters is that you should *never* have to read a letter twice. Usually, when you read mail more than once it's because you decided, on your first reading, that there wasn't anything urgent to be done. But why should a letter that's not important merit the time of a second reading?

You can avoid this sort of wasted effort by *always reading letters with a pencil in your hand*. If you need a response, jot down what you want to say directly on the letter. If the letter should be brought to the attention of someone else in your company, then write that person's name on it. If you need to discuss the letter with a group of people, then make a note of that. And as you make your notes put your letters in two different piles: Urgent and Can Wait. When you get back to these marked letters you'll only have to read your own notes rather than reevaluate the entire correspondence.

A friend of mine is an agent with one of New York's top literary agencies. He once saw me going through some letters and scribbling my usual notes, and said he had to fight a great urge to rip the pencil out of my hand. It seems that the library of his agency's offices is decorated with framed letters of some of their earliest and most famous clients. There are letters from Tolstoy, George Bernard Shaw, and Winston Churchill, and all of those framed letters have penciled notes in the margins and big pencil x's going through paragraphs.

The founder of the agency obviously knew that the best way to read a letter was with a pencil in his hand. Unfortunately, collectors of such letters probably feel faint every time they walk into the agency's library.

Confirmations

Never confirm appointments. It takes time to make those extra calls to clients and prospects and I usually find that I have better use for my time. When I make an appointment I let the person know that it's definite. I might say something like, "I'm writing this down in my calendar in ink," or "I'll be there for *sure.*" Don't ever say, "I won't be calling you to confirm this appointment," because you'll make it sound like you're not doing something you should be doing.

Meals

Always try to use mealtime for business. I've got a very tight schedule and I almost never eat a meal alone. Assuming that you're in an area of sales that requires meal-entertaining, you've got to take that responsibility very seriously.

Establish Your Own Set of Rules

Spend a week making notes on how you spend your time. When you look over your notes you'll be able to determine where most of your time gets wasted. At that point you'll have to set up rules.

One of my strictest rules involves the telephone. Whenever anyone calls my office and asks for me they're told I'm not in. Someone takes their name and number and I call them back when it fits into *my* schedule. I *never* accept phone calls.

That may sound a bit extreme to you but I've had years of experience with phone interruptions. Somehow what the person on the other end of the receiver considers "urgent" is rarely what I consider urgent. When I'm involved in something and stop to pick up the phone I don't just lose the time it takes for us to have our conversations; I lose the time it takes for me to let go of my train of thought and find it again.

I've found it helpful to set aside a certain time every day to talk to the people I work with and to do "telephone work." When that time of day rolls around I collect all of the messages I've received and sort them out. Some of the calls will be answered. Some of them will be put aside for a day. The point of all this is that it keeps me in control of my time. It is always *I* who decides how long, with whom, and when to be on the telephone.

I've also found it important to set limits on how long I'll wait for a friend. People are usually prompt for business appointments, but somehow when it came to friendly get-togethers, I found myself spending a great deal of time sitting alone at a table looking at my watch.

I decided finally that I wouldn't wait for anyone beyond fifteen minutes. I called all my friends and told them that I was very pressed for time and explained my new rule. Everyone understood, and with the exception of my brother, people usually make an effort to meet me within fifteen minutes of the time we've arranged.

My brother has learned to look at his watch when he's racing to meet me crosstown at a restaurant. As soon as his watch indicates that he's more than fifteen minutes late, he stops rushing.

The "Where Did I Put That?" Syndrome

The most common and consistent time-wasting activity is "looking for things." Most people who waste time are forever looking for things. The best antidote for that particular ailment is consistency. Try to establish special places for special things. Whenever I get a coat check, or a ticket from a garage, or any slip of paper that will have to be redeemed later that day, I put it in my right coat pocket. If, when I reach for it, the check isn't in that one specific pocket I don't even have to bother going through all my other pockets and my attaché case. I know that somehow or other I've managed to lose it. But when you have a specific place for things you'll begin to notice that you rarely lose them.

I once placed a woman with a paper manufacturer. Her job required a car, and a week after she started she called me hysterically at ten thirty in the morning. She had spent the last two hours looking for her car keys with no success, and couldn't get to her appointments. She'd already missed one meeting and was late for her second.

She found the keys that evening on a kitchen shelf, but she had lost an entire day of appointments by the time they turned up. I told her to get a hammer and a big nail and pound the nail into the wall just beside her door. From that day on, the moment she walked into her house she hung her keys on the nail. The motion of closing the door and hanging up her keys became one reflex movement so that she never had to question the location of her keys: they were either plugged into her dashboard or hanging from the nail.

Have Work Will Travel

Get in the habit of always carrying work with you. It's likely that at some point in the day things won't go precisely as you planned. You may have a meeting with someone who keeps you waiting for a half hour. He "can't help it." There was an "emergency." Whatever *his* problem may be it needn't become your problem if you've got some work with you.

Whenever you travel bring work along. If you end up circling Kennedy Airport for five hours you won't have to twiddle your thumbs. One of the main reasons that busy executives often have limousines is so that they can work comfortably in the back seat.

The Two-Hour Job

Every now and then you'll have some work to do that you know will take at least two hours. Your impulse, when you have that kind of work, will be to look for two free hours that you can afford to set aside. (If you've planned your schedule properly, you shouldn't even have two free hours!)

The best way to approach a two-hour job is to view it as six twenty-minute jobs. Learn to work in fifteen- or twenty-minute bursts. If you combine this advice with the idea of always bringing work with you when you travel, you're not likely to be wasting much time. You never know when you'll be caught in a cab for fifteen minutes, and you'll feel much more relaxed if you spend that time working, rather than watching the meter.

Who Gets Your Time

You never want to be in the position of spending vast amounts of time on low-yield accounts. I'm not suggesting that you be rude to your small accounts. Several of them combined may bring in the same amount of money as one big account. But just think about how much better you'd be doing with several big accounts. You have to use common sense. It's just not worth investing business time when you know the returns will be low. Your time is too valuable to be spent without forethought.

The Books for the System

Ideally everyone should have a flexible mind and a rigid schedule. Unfortunately it usually works out the other way around. I'm not sure what I can do to make your mind more flexible, but I'm convinced that I can help you establish a tighter schedule.

When I first started working I developed a system that I dubbed "the little pieces of paper system." Whenever someone called me I'd write down his name on a little piece of paper and put it in my pocket. On any given night there would be thirty or forty pieces of paper in my pocket, and invariably I'd get back to the people that weren't important and miss the ones that were. So I decided that my system needed refining.

I resolved to allocate pockets. My shirtfront pocket was for the very important messages, and my jacket pocket was for everything else. The problem with this new system was that every week when I got my shirts back from the laundry I discovered lots of lightly starched messages tucked away in the corners of my pockets!

My current system—although a bit mundane—has been working smoothly for the last nine years. The keys to this system are my books; and I've got several of them.

Week-at-a-Glance

My weekly appointment book is the backbone of my organizational system. With this sort of book, every time you open a page you see an entire week's scheduling at a glance. This kind of overview is important when you're planning with a tight schedule.

Every appointment I make is noted in this book, both social and business. I can account for literally all of my time during the last nine years by just going back over my nine books. I've also found it helpful to note the name *and* telephone number of my appointments. If ever I'm detained at one meeting and have to move my next meeting back, I want to be able to have all of the phone numbers I'll need at my fingertips.

It may take you a while to find the particular Week-at-a-Glance book that best suits your needs. They come in a variety of sizes and until you've had some experience arranging your schedule you won't really know how much space you'll need or how big a book you're comfortable carrying. I began with a tiny book that fit in my breast pocket and graduated to a book that requires my carrying an attaché case.

You may already be using a weekly appointment book or system. In most families it's the woman's responsibility to do most of the social planning. Women who have successfully juggled dinner dates with music lessons and cub scout meetings may have a calendar system that they can apply to their business life.

The Day-List Book

My second book is a simple secretary's stenographic pad. This book's purpose is to help coordinate my daily personal responsibilities with my business life.

I write a day of the week at the top of each page and make a list of everything that I have to do within that day. Some of the things on a given day will be directly transcribed from a prior day's list. But beyond those kinds of updatings, I try to think of everything else that I have to do on a given

day and write it down. The list can include the names of people I have to call, picking up my shirts at the laundry, mailing
in my rent, or sending someone a birthday card.

I also have an elaborate system of symbols that go along
with this day-list book. No one, other than myself, knows what
those symbols mean, and no one else needs to know what they
mean. But I know that when I do one of the chores on the
list I cross it out. When I call someone who isn't in, I make
a certain kind of squiggle next to that name. Everyone with
such a book can develop her own set of symbols.

At the end of the day I look through my list and assess
what has and hasn't been accomplished. At the same time I
make adjustments: I may move something from Wednesday
over to Friday; I may make a new note for any given day.

There's a hidden benefit to this sort of book. Personal
notebooks come in handy. Whenever I ask someone to do
something for me the request appears somewhere in my day-
list book. A week later when that person says, "But, David,
you never asked me to do that," I can check my book to see
whether I forgot to ask or he forgot to do. Being definite about
such things gives you firm ground to stand on if there's a con-
frontation brewing.

I have a very, very good memory, but I try never to rely
on it. If you have a good memory you should make a point of
not taxing it. The worst thing you can do is tell yourself, as
you're about to fall asleep, "I must remember to do such and
such tomorrow." The only thing that sort of message might
do is cost you a sound night's sleep.

The Telephone Directory

You'll save yourself a lot of time if you keep a complete
and detailed personal telephone directory.

Let me explain what I mean by "complete and detailed."
In my phone directory I have the name and address of anyone

with whom I'm likely to be in contact, as well as the name of his/her secretary. I always enter the address and phone number at the same time. If you don't do that you'll find that whenever you want to mail something you'll be missing the address, and whenever you want to call someone you'll be missing the number. It's guaranteed to work out conversely to your needs if you don't enter everything at the same time. (There's a rule of nature that governs the rain when you forget your umbrella, and the phone numbers when you need to make a call!)

The "If Lost in the Files" Book

Every now and then I forget how I filed something. I might have a letter from a sales manager at Prudential Insurance and be undecided as to where it should go: under his name, under "P" for Prudential, or under "I" for insurance. Usually when something like that happens I'm aware of the conflict and equally aware that it might cause problems at a later date.

Whenever I'm not sure where to file something I make a note in a little pad saying exactly where the slip of paper ended up. If I filed the Prudential letter under "P" but looked for it under the sales manager's name I'd just whip out my little book and clear up my confusion. If you don't rely heavily on files this book won't seem very important to you. If you do rely on a filing system, then you know what it's like to go through every single file in search of a piece of paper. When you finally find it, you understand exactly why you put it where you did . . . but that analysis isn't worth an hour and a half of your time.

The Dossiers

I have a manila folder on every client I ever had. Whenever I learn something about a client I put that information into my folder. If a client is into boating I make a note of it. If he has a sheepdog I note that. I write down a client's wife's name, children's names and schools, favorite drink—anything that will help me establish a relationship that's conducive to his buying. I honestly believe that women are better at remembering "personal data" than men. Talking about "the trip to Europe/the new boat/the country house" comes more naturally to many women than it does to men, but remember what I said earlier about not taxing your memory.

Besides personal data, my dossiers include briefings on meetings and phone conversations I've had with that particular client. Whenever I have a sales meeting, I write a note and put it in my file. Reading about what went on in your last meeting is good preparation for the meeting that's coming up.

If I pick up my dossier five minutes before I call my client I'll be prepared for a comfortable conversation. I might say, "Last time we talked you had just bought an eighteen-foot sailboat. How's it going?" That kind of attention is likely to take the pressure off a sales call and help you both to feel comfortable.

A woman I once placed with a pharmaceutical house followed my advice about dossiers but made a careless mistake once she got on the phone. She was flipping through her file when her client picked up. She said, "Hi! How are you? And how's Charlotte?" She had met the doctor's wife a few months earlier at a social gathering and was eager to reestablish the personal level of the contact. She looked down at her file and read that the client's wife's name was Paulette. She had no idea where she got the name Charlotte from. Before she had a chance to correct herself, her client blurted out, "My God! How did you know about Charlotte!"

So even with the best of systems you can make mistakes. The fact remains, however, that the better organized you are, the more smoothly your business will function. And the more smoothly your business functions, the more time you'll have.

Don't get the idea that I'm promoting a life-style that's 100 percent business. When you learn how to make the most of your time you'll have the space in your schedule for fun . . . whatever that means to you!

Shaping Up and Selling

Another, equally important, component in a program geared toward making the most of your time involves getting yourself into top shape—both physically and mentally. When you're tired, feeling ill or depressed, you're just not going to be able to move quickly.

I'm not about to prescribe a diet and exercise program for you. Our needs are all different. But I must stress the connection between keeping healthy and keeping productive. I can best use myself as an example.

For a very long time I took my low energy level for granted. Sure, there were people who had more energy than I, but I chalked that up to different metabolisms or different personalities. I figured that there wasn't much to be done about it. And I was dead wrong. Never assume that you have less energy than the next person because "that's just the way it is." Always try and figure out what accounts for the difference.

I recognized that I had to make some changes in order to get more work out of my workday. The first thing I had to do was stop smoking. Cigarette smoking made my chest feel heavy and generally dragged me down.

I also came to relate a number of other problems to my cigarette addiction. I've heard it suggested that the best way to break bad habits is to take them one at a time. First, stop smoking. Second, go on a diet. Third, stop biting your nails. But somehow when I looked at each of those problems individually they didn't seem like big enough problems for me to devote my energies to. In fact, I found it easier to do all three at once rather than one at a time. However you deal with bad habits, the important thing is to make a real effort. You'll find that you really do feel a lot better when you gain control of yourself.

The next thing I had to do was figure out a way to get eight hours of sleep every night. I learned that I couldn't function as well on three or four hours of sleep as I did on eight. My clients could tell the difference.

The first thing I did was try to limit my socializing to Friday and Saturday nights. If I went out socially on a weekday night I allowed myself to sleep the full eight hours. After a few such instances of arriving at my office at noon I developed enough of a guilty conscience to avoid repeat performances. I stuck to the weekends and I got home early on weeknights.

I also discovered that I was not, by anyone's definition, a "good drinker." I was never able to drink a lot. So I stopped drinking during my workweek. During the week my sole priority was to function well for my work.

With all of these changes I was feeling pretty good. I lost five pounds, my urges to put my fingers or a cigarette in my mouth were eliminated, and I was feeling considerably more energetic. I moved a step further with my program.

I decided to begin exercising. Physical exercise not only builds your body but also gets oxygen into your body. That oxygen is a source of energy, and no matter how loath you are to begin exercising, you'll feel great once you get into a routine. It will reflect in your work output.

Finally, I read a book called *Sugar Blues*. After I read the book I identified sugar as my number one enemy. Nutritionally it gave me nothing. And it's responsible for everything from varicose veins to baggy eyes to poor complexion to diabetes. Even if you're one of those extraordinary individuals who "can eat anything and never gain a pound," you'd probably feel a lot more energetic if you did away with sugar.

Mental Attitudes

Obviously, your attitude will affect your performance. You have to accept, for example, that you will never make fifteen sales for every fifteen calls you make. Once you accept the fact that not everyone is going to buy your product/service, you'll have conquered the biggest problem of most beginning salesmen: FEAR OF REJECTION.

I maintain that there is no rejection in sales. Essentially, you have to come to recognize that when someone chooses to not buy your product/service, it has nothing to do with you. When you ask someone to buy something and they decline your offer, the *least* likely reason for their refusal is that they don't like you. The most likely reason for their refusal is that they don't need what you're offering. It may be that they can't get approval to buy your product. Whatever their reason for saying "No," you can't dwell on it. If you get depressed every time someone chooses not to buy, you'll find yourself feeling very tired. After a while you may not even feel like making appointments.

A depressed attitude in sales can use up a lot of time. It can, in fact, use up your life. If you find yourself feeling depressed because people haven't been buying, or haven't been returning phone calls, I suggest that you schedule yourself two weeks in advance as tightly as possible. A busy schedule is the best protection against disappointment. Sometime within your busy two weeks you'll make a sale. And as a saleswoman, there's nothing better that you can do with your time than SELL.

It's important to note that all of the time-organizing techniques that I've discussed here can be applied to almost any profession or life-style. Planning implies a certain degree of relaxation, and that kind of relaxation is nice to have . . . whatever you do.

CHAPTER

12

Sex

When you're in a people business and most of those people are of the opposite sex, sooner or later you'll have to deal with sex. The most important thing for you to remember about clients and sex is that the two must never be mixed. Never, under any circumstances, should you enter into a sexual relationship with a client. If you meet a client who you know is going to be the most important man in your life—the man you've been waiting for—and if he feels the same way about you, then you should give his account over to someone else on your sales force before you add a new, complicated dimension to your relationship.

Until you are absolutely clear that you will not fraternize with any clients, you're going to have a difficult time dealing with their advances. To be sure, the advances will come. They needn't, however, pose a problem. If you're clear on where you stand (which is to remain standing) there are ways to give them that message and still maintain a professional relationship.

I don't think it's important for me to delve into all of the reasons why you shouldn't become sexually involved with a client. Suffice it to say that sexual relationships carry the potential of pressure and confusion. Business relationships also carry that potential, and neither kind of relationship needs the added complication of a double dose of pressure or confusion. If you know that you're the kind of woman who can handle a "casual" affair without any ramifications, that's fine for you. But you must accept the fact that you are in a very small minority. It's not likely—and it certainly shouldn't be assumed —that your client/lover can do the same thing. No matter what he says.

The Sexy Society

We're all living in a very sexy society. In the old days, treating a woman with respect and not engaging her in any sexual activity were synonymous. It was reasonable for a woman to feel insulted if a man directed a sexual overture in her direction.

Today, sex is everywhere. Everyone's thinking about it. There are pictures of people half-naked on billboards. There are pictures of people entirely naked in magazines. It's the focus of advertising. There's an enormous amount of time spent on the activities of matching, meeting, mating and marriage. Sex is the subject of the day.

Given this environment of sexual permissiveness, it's no longer an insult to your respectability if a man makes a pass at you. Of course, I'm not saying you should enjoy being harassed by men as you walk down your city's streets. In fact, I'm not saying that you should enjoy being *harassed* by men anywhere. But you'll do a lot better in the business world if you don't interpret a come-on by an otherwise respectable man as an insult.

Just how do you interpret it? I think you'll be making

life a lot easier for yourself if you assume that when a guy makes a sexual advance he's paying you a compliment. He's saying, "I am personally attracted to you." Unfortunately, many men are heavy-handed when they make advances. They may be crude or awkward, but the message is the same from those men as it is from a man with more polish. No matter how they say it, they're saying that they find you attractive.

You may recall earlier that I said it was your job to consider your client's psychological position. If a client is late you should respond with understanding. Your goal is to make a sale—regardless of your client's punctuality.

The same rule applies to men making sexual advances. You may not feel very sympathetic to a man coming on to you, but let me tell you how that man feels. I've already explained that he feels attracted to you. Yet he also feels nervous about expressing that attraction. Women may have grown up in the position of sitting by the telephone, but men grew up having to make phone calls and anticipate rejection. It's not a lot of fun to ask a woman out and be told, "I'm sorry but you're too young/old/short/tall/fat/skinny."

To some degree every man who makes a pass feels a bit of the same anxiety that he felt in high school when he called to make his first date. If you feel insulted by a man's sexual attention you're likely to say, "I hate the idea of men always out to make a move," or something like that. That sort of rebuff goes right to a man's ego and hurts. No man with a hurt ego is going to want to see you to discuss business. In fact, he's not going to want to see you at all. He feels like a fool in your presence.

The Rebuff

What do you do if you're advised not to sleep with a man, and not to hurt his ego? You have to learn to rebuff someone *nicely*. A *nice* rebuff means that you thank him for his attention, you make his ego feel good and you go on to business. Consider the following situation.

You call up a client you've met once, several months earlier. You say that you think it's time for the two of you to get together again and would he be free for a lunch? He responds, "I'm pretty busy for lunch, but how about dinner or breakfast. Or even better, how about dinner followed by breakfast with a very slight interruption?" And then he'll laugh.

That, in case you missed it, is a pass. The fact that this pass is disguised as "some kidding" doesn't make it any less a pass. Most first passes are disguised by kidding and *must* be responded to with a nice rebuff.

A nice rebuff to the above pass would be, "Ah! If only our paths had crossed four years earlier, before I met the love of my life, that might have been an attractive offer." Another nice rebuff would be, "If I were going to mix business and pleasure with anyone, it would surely be you. But there *is* my cardinal rule, which is my only religious conviction—that I don't mix the two." One more might be, "It would be nice, but I have a boyfriend who feels about me the way you'd probably feel about your girlfriend/wife. So let's make it lunch, or breakfast, or dinner, but in either case, let's make it business. And let's be friends."

Each of the above rebuffs says that the reason you're turning him down isn't because of *him*. It's because of a social contract, or a personal conviction, and you're making a point of allowing him out gracefully.

Only Kidding

Most first moves come in the guise of "friendly kidding." If, as I've suggested above, you keep the tone light, you shouldn't have any problem moving on to business. In fact, the reason that most men will initiate the subject of sex in a "kidding" context is that they want to save their pride. If you rebuff them they can always say, "Hey. Wait a minute there. I was only kidding."

But, as I said earlier, kidding is a signal. It's part of an elaborate mating dance that we're all involved in. We test the water. We use some innuendo. We touch a woman's elbow. All of those subtle (or not so subtle) moves should be read by a businesswoman as *signals,* and if you deal with those signals while they're still just that, you won't have problems later.

Signal to Signal

Very often a sexual "problem" in business can become unmanageable because a woman doesn't deal with it while it's still in the signal stage of development. Instead of sending back her own codified message (which should translate into "You're a great guy but this relationship is going to be strictly business") some women decide to put the pass aside for a while and go on with business.

I once placed a woman in industrial sales. Since that field is predominantly male, it was clear that she was going to have to deal with the issue of sex. Finally, when an important client of hers suggested they spend a weekend together at his beach house, she said, "That's an exciting offer. I'd better not think about it now, however. I need to get back to business."

That worked for a few weeks until the offer came up again. Again she put her client off. The third time he made his offer he was anticipating her response, and he was angry. In essence, the saleswoman kept telling him "Maybe." She was leading him on, and after a while he felt like he was being teased. If you keep saying "Maybe" the average man's interest is going to be fired up. He'll feel like he's being strung along. No one enjoys that feeling.

The best thing you can do when you sense that a client is coming on to you is to be firm, consistent, definite and *nice.* (Don't ever forget "nice.") Usually when women raise their hands at my seminars and say, "What do you do if . . . ?" they're giving me a problem that could have been avoided if they had dealt with it earlier. If you give a clear negative signal from the start, most men will back off.

About Your Signals

Some women never have problems with men, not because they're unattractive but because their very deportment indicates that they aren't open to sexual advances. If you present yourself in a totally professional manner you'll avoid a lot of problems.

Not too long ago I went to a convention in Las Vegas. The meeting was hosted by a manufacturer and they invited several of their clients to attend and learn about their product. Also in attendance was the sales force: twenty-five men and fifteen women. After the meeting the manufacturer hosted a party in a disco. A number of women got up on the dance floor and really did some torrid numbers—with bumps and grinds and little left to the imagination. Those women, without saying a word, were creating a problem for themselves. They might just as well have hung up a sign that said, "I'm a number."

You should also make it a point not to discuss your personal life with clients. If you open up your personal life to them they'll feel that they have a right to tread there. If, on the other hand, you keep your relationship warm, friendly and *professional,* you'll avoid any confusion.

The Myths and the Realities

Sales is not the raunchy end of business that concerns itself with providing prostitutes and dirty jokes. It may be true that some salesmen have chosen to operate in that milieu, but that's a matter of choice. Anyone who tells you that you *must* get involved in sex in order to sell is someone you shouldn't trust. It's just not true.

You might also keep in mind that *men* have promoted the myth that women wouldn't be able to handle the "sex" end of sales. The men most adamant about that stand are, in fact, the men most threatened by your presence in the business world. It's a scare tactic and you have no reason to be scared.

Nor should you act like the woman who's seen it all and done it all. Don't try to prove to men that they can't shock you. It will only give them an incentive to try. You can sound mature, sophisticated and professional without sounding like you've "seen a lot of hard miles."

If you ever do encounter a man who won't leave you alone, who won't take a hint, or who won't keep his hands off you, you shouldn't feel at all uncomfortable about contacting his superior and informing your boss of the problem. It's very unusual for a man not to respond to early warning signals from you, and if he doesn't, it's an indication that he has problems. Remember, they're *his* problems, not *yours*.

What If You Didn't Act Soon Enough?

All of this advice is fine if you're just beginning. But what if you've been selling for a while and are embroiled in lots of client problems that are rooted in sex? I don't have much advice for women who *did* get sexually involved with clients and who are finding that their sexual relationships have gone sour. The best I can suggest is that you extricate yourself either from the affair, from the saleswoman—client relationship, or from both. And don't let it happen again.

If, on the other hand, you've been putting someone's sexual advances aside, like the woman I placed in industrial sales, you're going to have to deal with them the next time they come up. I suggest that you begin with an apology and then go on to explain with a nice—with an extra-nice—rebuff. The most important thing at that point is that you are firm and consistent. Don't leave the matter of a sexual relationship between you open. Close the door, and don't close it on his foot.

It may seem to you like that sort of interaction is terribly difficult. In fact, it's not. Given the fact that your client has approached you, you can assume that he's approached other women in his professional life. You won't be the first woman to say "No," and he'll probably want to make it as easy as possible for you and for himself.

PART
4

The Selling Women

Sylvia Krutech—Advertising Space

Sylvia Krutech, at forty-one, is the mother of two chil-dren, a seventeen-year-old son and a fifteen-year-old daughter. Four years ago her marriage of fourteen years ended in divorce. She was left with a house in one of New York's affluent suburbs and very little in the way of prac-tical, work-applicable experience. She was placed by Ca-reers For Women at The Institutional Investor *where she's been selling advertising space for the last three years. Re-cently she was made a manager and her salary shot from $13,000 her first year to $25,000 her third. Next year she anticipates that her income will exceed $30,000.*

My life has changed so extraordinarily since I got in-volved in sales that I almost don't know where to begin. Before I got into sales I was a recently divorced woman with a B.S. in Education and a little bit of substitute teaching under my belt. I'd worked with organizations and done a lot of tennis playing. I fell upon Careers For Women when I began to search for a way to become gainfully employed.

I learned to sell advertising space almost three years ago on my first job. The work was exciting and rewarding, but even more exciting was the fact that I began to develop a whole new self-image as a capable and productive working woman. After two years with my company I was promoted to Eastern Sales Manager. I suppose that because I see the op-portunities for myself opening up in a way I never would have imagined five years ago, I feel very, very excited about my fu-

235

ture. I've come to realize that one can get back into the business world even after many years of being home and raising a family.

I particularly love my job because I see myself primarily as a people-person. I love to be out and meeting people and would probably not be very well suited for a restricting office-type job. Oddly enough, I see my teaching career as having been helpful to me in sales. Basically I try to educate a potential advertiser as to the merits of my publication as well as helping him to solve problems.

I suppose the very hardest aspect of selling advertising space is learning not to overeat at lunch—unless you've got the metabolism of a hummingbird!

Debbie Flanz—Dun & Bradstreet

Debbie Flanz lives in her own apartment in Manhattan. She's twenty-four years old, and with the exception of working in her family's business at home in Michigan, selling Dun & Bradstreet's financial service is her first job. Her first year's base salary is $13,000 but she's been guaranteed that her minimum earnings this year will be $18,000.

I went to the University of Michigan, got my degree, and then spent several years traveling in Europe before I got into sales. When I got out of college I was unsure of how to utilize my talents. I like business, law, and being creative, so when I got back from Europe I started working in my family business. I'd worked there before college as well.

The sales aspect of the business interested me. I knew that it was the real heart of the business and I enjoyed getting very involved in it. Then I decided to come to New York and go on my own, and I found my work with Dun & Bradstreet's intangibles service even more creative and interesting.

I have a territory in Manhattan and I cover all the commercial business within that area. I go to businessmen and help them deal with their accounts receivable programs. I show them what cash flow is, depending on how sophisticated their business is, and I try to sell them a service which collects money on commercial accounts.

My life has changed immensely since I got into sales. I have a keener business sense than I had before. Growing up in a business family I suppose you get a lot of education by osmosis, and then for four years I studied business and economics in school, but all of that was somehow abstract. When you walk into a prospect's office it's not abstract anymore. You've got to go for their needs quickly. You have to *see* what they want and *feel* what they're saying. You're dealing with them on a one-to-one basis, which is what I like most about my work.

I remember one particular woman by the name of Rose Augustine who manufactured nylon strings for stringed instruments. It's incredible to sit down and talk to somebody like her—to look at her accounts and see how she makes money. At the same time I got to talk about her art collection, about how she tied a degree in chemistry in with a career as a concert pianist and how she eventually formed a business like the one she has. It gives me a good perspective in which to think about my own life.

I'm basically an entrepreneurial person. I think it's something I was born with. The work I'm doing now is giving me an overview of business. I'm learning about credit, about law, and it all excites me. I know all of this information will be useful to me in future entrepreneurial steps.

I love variety in life. It keeps me going. Working in sales

has provided me with that, as well as with independence. I like to organize, to set my own schedules, and to work within my own territory. It's like my own business. That's all.

LaQuita Henry–Essence

LaQuita Henry is twenty-eight years old and has had a varied work experience. She's single and has her own apartment in Manhattan. She's ambitious and likes to make a good living, and has earned just under $25,000 during her first year in advertising space sales.

After I got my master's in International Affairs from Columbia University I taught for a year and a half. I was dissatisfied with teaching and a friend told me about a job doing business research for a nonprofit urban research organization. While I was there I heard about a job heading up marketing and research for a merchandising firm, and I decided that I was definitely interested in pursuing a career in business.

In the course of my business research I had met with heads of small, predominantly black businesses, and I got a sense of what determined success or failure in a business. The research I did in this second job was very different from the first in that it gave me more of an overview of business. I also assisted my boss on sales presentations, and that left me feeling sort of bad. I was only delivering the research and I felt left out. I wanted to develop and to do more. I also wanted to start making money for myself. It's nice to get business experience, but you also need to feed your face.

I found out about Careers For Women, and through them I interviewed for the job at *Essence*. Sure enough, I was genuinely intrigued by sales—especially for a magazine. It's a very glamorous job, and I like that kind of life-style.

Really, my involvement in sales has improved my life. I

enjoy meeting people. I'm still a little bit anxious about having first meetings, but I feel a lot more confident. I'm not afraid. And I like the kind of persuading that's involved in convincing someone to buy your product. I like going to conventions and traveling with my company. It's a very, very busy, hectic kind of job that requires a lot of reading, lots of letter writing, and keeping up with what's going on.

It often seems that there's not enough time in the day, and not enough days in the week to actually do all the things that I want. Sometimes the pressure can get me a little bit down—if I don't break a big account that I was after—but generally I like the fast pace.

Sales is terrifically exciting. It helps you learn an awful lot about yourself—what you can take, what you like, and what you don't like. And it helps you learn about people. You learn how to size a person up and how to tell about their character after three minutes.

That knowledge extends beyond your actual job. You take it with you into every aspect of your life.

Anita Smith–Allstate Air Cargo

Anita Smith lives with her husband in Leonia, New Jersey. She's thirty-seven years old and has three step-children aged twenty-one, eighteen, and thirteen. She's been involved in sales for only five months and estimates that her first year's salary will exceed $14,000, and that her second year's income will be at least 25 percent higher than that.

I've always enjoyed working with people. Before I got into sales I taught my own classes in cosmetics and grooming at a high school in Morris County, New Jersey. I based my classes on the work I had done as grooming supervisor for Overseas National Airways where I taught all the classes for new flight attendants, both male and female. Before that I was assistant director for a modeling school.

Through my work in sales I've discovered that I have much more potential than I ever realized. In the four months since I've been working at Allstate Air Cargo I've created many new accounts. I haven't gotten all the accounts I've gone out for, but nobody does. I'm still working on some big ones. But I'm confident that the harder I work, the more I'll achieve, and I like to sit down at the end of the week and say, "I really had a good week," or "Gee, it wasn't such a good week because of this, that and the other thing. So far, I've had the most new accounts for three of my first four months on the job, which means an extra check. That's always a good boost for the ego and the pocketbook.

I'm very, very pleased with the work that I'm doing, and I enjoy feeling like I'm good at it. I also enjoy knowing that I have good earning potential. I love the fact that I'm not tied to a time clock, and I always get to meet a great variety of people—which means I always face new challenges. It's very important to me to feel that I'm able to stand on my own two feet. Sales has assured me of that!

Janet Fanshawe—Continental Can

Janet Fanshawe is twenty-five years old, single, and lives in her own apartment on Manhattan's Upper West Side. She did a great deal of personal research before she got involved in industrial sales and feels like her effort has paid off. In her first year at Continental Can she earned a salary of $20,000, plus a $3,000 bonus, a company *car, and a liberal expense account. All of that computes to a first-year earnings of close to $30,000. Next year she expects to do significantly better.*

When I was in college I concentrated in Marketing Research, and I assumed that I'd be working in that area. But when I began to go on job interviews I discovered that with a specialty in marketing and research you sit at a desk for about eight years with a calculator and work out percentages. You don't get to go to a store, meet anybody, or do anything that requires contact with people. After a while I recognized that I didn't want to do what I had been preparing for.

The agency I'd been interviewing through suggested I get involved in sales, and I interviewed with the Dale Carnegie Institute. For two years I sold the Carnegie Development Program to corporations. It was helpful to me because in order to sell the program you have to take the classes yourself, and I actually developed while I was selling development. Those two years also enabled me to meet people in management and sales and all the basic areas of business, from secretaries up to presidents of companies. They all discussed their work problems with me and I got a real sense of what was exciting and what wasn't as glamorous as it appeared.

But I was working long hours, not making much money, and I didn't have any real promotional opportunities, so I began to look again. I came to Careers For Women knowing that I wanted sales, but not certain of which area of business I was interested in. The job at Continental Can was appealing on a number of levels.

First, they wanted me to sell a new product—the new two-liter plastic beverage bottles. I came in early on the product's history, which meant that I could couple practical sense with really creative selling. I'd call on bottlers like Coke, 7-Up and Pepsi, and talk with them and work with them and hope that I'd get their business rather than my competition. In January my company sent me to California for five months to do things out there. Now I'm back in the Northeast and I travel two or three days a week.

Working at a company like Continental Can offered an interesting challenge. It's an essentially male population and most of the men are a bit older, recruited from the Ivy League, and very conservative. I had to learn how to be the only woman. It worked out really well, and I'd say that my future is not only in sales, but in management as well.

I work on developing a sale, but I also work on developing programs that I think might help. There's a tremendous amount of interfacing in departments at a management level, so you always see how your work fits into the whole. You can work with technical people, with business people, and see a concept as it develops. That sort of interfacing is giving me an overview of business and helping me see what parts of management I'd like to get involved in.

My next step is into National Accounts, which has a title of manager because it involves a lot of administration. I still haven't refined my future goals, but I'm in an exciting position to determine, for myself, what I want to be doing.

Aurora Tandberg–New York Life

Aurora Tandberg has been selling life insurance for six years, during which her income has skyrocketed from $28,000 to $50,000 a year. She is thirty-two years old, divorced, and owns her own home in Tom's River, New Jersey.

Prior to joining New York Life I spent ten years in banking. I started as a secretary and worked my way up first to

Assistant Manager, and then to a corporate officer. As a corporate officer I was in charge of a branch and responsible for servicing customers. I worked very hard, and while I enjoyed the people I worked with, I earned all of $12,000 a year. Someone else controlled my income and my future.

Sales has given me a whole new perspective on life. It gave me the opportunity to grow as an individual. The challenge it presents allows me to constantly set higher goals for myself, and I feel very proud when I achieve them. It's a good feeling to be in control of your own life.

The income I've earned in the last six years has given me freedom. People say that money isn't everything, but it certainly gives you the opportunity of self-determination. I don't *have* to be married. I don't *have* to be with a person just because of financial security. I provide my own security, and when I'm with somebody else it's because I *want* to be, not because I have to be. It's provided the basis for much healthier relationships.

By the time I'm thirty-five I'd like to have my own sales office. At my current rate of income growth I expect to be earning at least $100,000 at that point, which will make it feasible for me to go out on my own. I like the idea of having my own agency because I love helping other people wake up to what they have inside them. And I think that you can do this through sales management. It's a great feeling to take a neophyte salesperson and bring them to the point where they're a professional . . . to see a real life-style change. I find it fascinating to see them go out and buy a house, or to feel the freedom and independence that I feel. That's the most exciting part of what I do.

So I see a very healthy, good and exciting future for myself. Every day is different. That's the beauty of sales. I don't think any career can offer you the same thing. It affords you personal growth, a great deal of interaction with people, and a chance to be independent. I love that.

Linda Smith–Lanier Business Products

Linda Smith is twenty-six years old and lives in Wald-wick, New Jersey. She's been married for four years. Her husband, also in business, is assistant to the president of a company that manufactures industrial tools. Linda has been involved in sales for a bit over a year and made $17,000 during her first year with Lanier. Based on the sales she's already made during her second year she esti-mates that she'll earn a minimum of $32,000. Although she has four and a half years' worth of college credits, Linda has not actually earned a college degree.

Before I went into sales I had about nine jobs in seven years covering everything from clerk typist to being the as-sistant to the president of a small consulting firm. Since my involvement in sales my life has changed in many ways. I feel gratified by the work I do on a day-to-day basis, and I'm a much happier person generally.

Sales has done a lot to develop my self-image. I feel com-petent, self-assured, very strong, and in control of my life. Specifically my job entails selling dictation machines—and word processing equipment—to forty major accounts with Fortune 100 companies. I call on everyone from heads of de-partments to presidents of companies, to purchasing agents. I hire and instruct secretaries on the use of my equipment, and I also instruct executives and people at a management level who will be using my machinery.

I very much like the type of people my job enables me to come in contact with. They're very dynamic, very aggres-sive, sharp and professional. I'm a real egomaniac, to be per-fectly blunt, and I enjoy the ego-feedback I get. I enjoy seeing how people feel about what I do for them on a personal basis.

I like the image that I project, and I like the way people respond to it. The company I keep is very important to me.

I'm not sure that I want to remain in the area of selling hard equipment. I'd like to feel more of a real personal commitment or involvement with my product than I do with dictation systems. But I'm very happy with my company and feel confident that I have a future with them if I want it. Selling "hardware" in New York is probably the toughest thing I could do, and everything from this point on is going to be gravy, easy and fun.

I see an open door ahead of me in terms of my working life. I can walk through and do anything I want. I know that I'm very desirable on the marketplace, and with a little specific preparation in a given field I can get in anywhere. It's going to be strictly my own choice!

Mary Salerno–Berley & Co.

Mary Salerno is forty-four years old and a native New Yorker. She lived in New Jersey when she was married, and moved back into Manhattan after her divorce. She works for one of the biggest commercial real estate companies in the city and has seen her salary increase from $16,000 to $25,000 to an anticipated $35,000 during her three years with them.

I used to be an executive secretary. That's how I started off. I worked for a man who was the president of a paper company for around ten years, and he died very suddenly. There was a great deal of turmoil and I was the only one in the company who really had any knowledge about what was going on in both the sales end of it and the paper end of it. I learned a great deal from having worked with him for so long about how to make paper, how to price it, and what the different kinds of paper could do.

There I was. A sales manager from our mill in Massachusetts came to the New York offices and he thought very highly of me. I mentioned that I wanted to do something in sales and that I didn't understand why they didn't use women in sales and he said, essentially, "Go ahead." I'd been doing it for years anyway and they were happy to have me. At that point I was in my late twenties, and I was making a respectable salary for a secretary, but it wasn't any money to speak of. Actually, I was the first woman in the paper industry to sell. They used to call me a salesman, but I didn't care. As long as I could do my work well.

Unfortunately the company moved its offices to Massachusetts, and I didn't want to move with them. I tried, for a while, to get another job in the paper industry but no one would hire a woman. They'd say, "Yes, we know you. We know you have a reputation and we know you've done beautifully, but if I hired you I'd have my throat slit by the men in our company."

I finally gave up and got another secretarial job working for the president of a labor relations firm. This firm handled many of the biggest Fortune 500 companies, and I learned a great deal about negotiating while I worked there.

Now I'm the Director of Office Leasing in our company, and I was the first saleswoman that Berley & Co. ever hired in 1975. David came to me and said that he thought I'd be terrific at real estate because of my negotiating experience, and in fact that experience has really paid off.

This job seemed to work well for me right from the beginning. I loved it. I loved the negotiating and the running and constant busy pace. I have a lot of energy, which is really important in this business. You need every bit of it you've got, and more. In fact, I was taking iron pills for a while. But I thrive on the pace.

I just got a college degree from Fordham—I was going at night—and I'm in the process of studying for my broker's license at New York University. Once I get that I'll be in a position to be made a vice-president, and I feel that I have a lot to look forward to.

GLOSSARY

Advance—That amount of money a company gives you which is guaranteed as your income. When you sell enough of your product to equal your advance you earn commission above the advance.

Banquette seating—Side-by-side seating in a restaurant as opposed to opposite (or face-to-face) seating. Banquette seating is considered less desirable on a business lunch.

Carry-over-minus—If your draw from a company exceeds the commission you've earned in any given year, theoretically a salesperson will begin the new year in a minus status. Hence, if you had a draw of $10,000 and earned a $1 commission for every item you've sold, you'd have to sell 10,000 items to earn out your draw. In a carry-over-minus situation if you've only sold 9,000 items you'll go into your new year with a $1,000 deficit. If, during that year you sell 11,000 items, you will only break even. Usually the employer will waive the technical minus and permit the salesperson to start the new year "even." This waiver will help to motivate the salesperson.

Chronological résumé—A résumé in which your work and educational experiences are listed chronologically starting with the present, and working back in time. Recommended résumé format for sales positions.

Close—The part of your sales presentation in which you determine whether or not your client is going to buy your product.

Cold calling—Arriving at the premises of a prospect without a prearranged appointment.

Consumer book (or publication)—A magazine of general interest such as the ones sold in drugstores or newsstands (i.e., *Cosmopolitan, Ladies' Home Journal, Reader's Digest, Esquire*, etc.).

Discretionary bonus—A nonspecific bonus determined by the sales manager or your superior based on his/her feelings about the effort and/or results of your work.

Earn-out figure—The number of items you must sell, or the amount of money you must earn for the company, before you begin to earn a commission over your advance. Also called "break-even figure."

Flat salary—No incentive (commission or bonus) above a regularly paid, guaranteed salary.

Incentive payment—Any form of bonus or commission. Money earned in specific relation to sales as opposed to a guaranteed salary.

Lead—A person who has expressed interest in your product.

Line promotions—Promotions that have line (profit-making) responsibilities rather than maintenance (spending) responsibilities. If your job brings money in to the company, it is a line job.

Media buyer—The person in an advertising agency who decides how to spend the predetermined media budget—where to spend the allocated amounts of money on print advertising, television advertising, etc. If you sell advertising space, your job is to convince a media buyer that his "print" money would be best spent by advertising in your publication.

Media planner—The person in an advertising agency who determines which media would be most effective to sell a product. He/she also determines the budget for advertising in specific media. The advertising space saleswoman may have some impact in determining how much money is allocated to "print" advertising if she meets with the media planner at the beginning of a campaign.

Nonrecriminatory draw—An advance against future commissions. The purpose of this advance is to provide the salesperson with a regularly paid income. In the nonrecriminatory draw situation the draw is the same thing as an "advance." It is a guaranteed part of the remuneration package. If the saleswoman does not sell enough merchandise to earn-out her draw she doesn't owe the company anything. In such arrangements you should not have to sign any agreement of liability.

Preferred seating—The section of a restaurant that is most preferred by regular diners.

Prospect—A potential customer.

Purchasing agent—Someone who has the responsibility for purchasing goods or services for a corporation, school district, etc.

Recriminatory draw—An advance against future commissions. If the salesperson does not earn the equivalent of the advance in future commissions she will owe her employer the balance of what she was paid, less what she earned. In order for such a situation to be legally binding you will have to sign an agreement of liability which says that your advance is actually no more than a loan. Under no circumstances should you agree to this situation or sign any document that treats a draw like a loan.

Saleswoman—A woman who sells something. (Just in case someone tells you, "You don't look like a saleswoman.")

Staff promotions—Promotions into jobs that don't actually bring money into a corporation but, rather, maintain the corporation's functioning (i.e., personnel, accounting, etc.).

Straight commission—No guaranteed amount of income. Salesperson is paid a percentage (commission) on gross sales.

Trade book (or publication)—A magazine with special interest for/within a given industry. Such publications are not available to general consumers.

INDEX